Games That Teach Teams

Games That Teach Teams

. . . .

21
ACTIVITIES
TO SUPER-CHARGE
YOUR GROUP!

STEVE SUGAR & GEORGE TAKACS

Jossey-Bass
Pfeiffer
San Francisco

ISBN: 0-7879-4835-7

Library of Congress Cataloging-in-Publication Data

Sugar, Steve.
Games that teach teams : 21 activities to super-charge your
group! / Steve Sugar and George Takacs.
p. cm.
Includes bibliographical references (p.) and index. ISBN
0-7879-4835-7 (alk. paper)
1. Management games. 2. Organizational learning. 3.
Employees--Training of. I. Takacs, George. II. Title. III. Title: 21
activities to super-charge your group!
HD30.26 .S842 2000
658.3'124--dc21   99-6684

The materials that appear in this book *(except those for which reprint permission must be obtained from the primary sources)* may be freely reproduced for educational/training activities. There is no requirement to obtain special permission for such uses. We do, however, ask that the following statement appear on all reproductions:

> *Games That Teach Teams: 21 Activities to Super-Charge Your Group!* by Steve Sugar and George Takacs. Copyright © 2000 by Jossey-Bass/Pfeiffer, San Francisco, CA.

This permission statement is limited to the reproduction of material for educational/training events. *Systematic or large-scale reproduction or distribution (more than one hundred copies per year)—or inclusion of items in publications for sale—may be done only with prior written permission. Also, reproduction on computer disk or by any other electronic means requires prior written permission.*

Printed in the United States of America

Published by

350 Sansome Street, 5th Floor
San Francisco, California 94104-1342
(415) 433-1740; Fax (415) 433-0499
(800) 274-4434; Fax (800) 569-0443

Visit our website at: www.pfeiffer.com

Acquiring Editor: Matthew Holt
Director of Development: Kathleen Dolan Davies
Developmental Editor: Susan Rachmeler
Editor: Rebecca Taff
Senior Production Editor: Dawn Kilgore
Manufacturing Supervisor: Becky Carreño
Interior Design & Illustrations: Gene Crofts
Cover Design: Brenda Duke

Printing 10   9   8   7   6   5   4   3   2   1

 This book is printed on acid-free, recycled stock that meets or exceeds the minimum GPO and EPA requirements for recycled paper.

Dedications

• •

This book is dedicated to Julius, Elma, and Linda Takacs
who encouraged intellectual curiosity and nurtured new ways
to approach reality.

George Takacs

To my family and friends, especially Marie,
who were always kind and feigned interest
as I rambled on about games.

Steve Sugar

Contents

• •

Preface   ix

Acknowledgments   xi

Part One
SETTING THE STAGE

Chapter One: What Is a Team?   3

Chapter Two: Building a Team   7

Chapter Three: Facilitation   19

Chapter Four: Team Games   33

Part Two
TWENTY-ONE TEAM GAMES

Book at a Glance   47

Bell Hop   51

Box of Chocolates   57

Brain Frame   63

Buzz Word   71

Cross Roads   83

Duel Identity   91

High Five 103

Line Up 107

Match Point 115

Name That Team 125

Norman Says! 131

Pass the Buck 139

Power Tag 145

RAT Race 151

Regards 173

Sentence Prompt 177

Snow Ball 183

Super Model 189

Team Roast 201

Tooth and Nail 207

ww.where and ww.when 217

About the Authors 225

Preface

• •

Building a team is not an easy job, for our Western culture idealizes the self-made man or woman and celebrates people doing things their own way and following their own dreams.

Building a team in a culture that holds, in law and symbol, the individual and his or her freedom and rights in such high esteem takes considerable time and effort. To build a team is really a continuing effort to build a team—not once, but over and over again.

This book is designed as a working reference to help you with the task of building, maintaining, and re-building a team. First, we "set the stage" by establishing guidelines in Chapters One and Two, "What Is a Team?" and "Building a Team." The stage continues to be set as we present tips on conducting your game in Chapters Three and Four, "Facilitation" and "Team Games." Next, we present a matrix, "Book at a Glance," that can be used to select the appropriate game in terms of skill(s) or knowledge you wish to teach to a specific type of team. Then we present twenty-one games that can be used in your team-building activities.

The major portion of the book is, of course, devoted to team games and activities that can be used with teams that are just forming and with teams that have been working together for awhile. Because the needs of each team are different, we have tried to meet those needs with a variety of games for use in a variety of circumstances. We take you through the steps of how each game is played and provide value-added comments on customizing the game for your audience and your needs. Please note that each game has a section, "Facilitator Notes," that gives valuable insight on how to play and process the game, including how to play the game with "cyber" teams. In each game we also provide "Player Instruction" sheets for overhead reproduction and, when necessary, provide sample rounds of play, game sheets, answer sheets, inventories, group process sheets, and lecture notes.

In short, we have tried to supply you with all the information you need to be a successful team builder. We only wish we had had this type of information earlier in our careers. But, then, that's why we wanted to write this book—to make your job of team building easier through our exercises and games.

Best success!

Acknowledgments

· ·

We would like to acknowledge colleagues who provided ideas and help with the following games:

- Duel Identity: Steve Grovender

- Power Tag: Arleen La Bella

- Regards: Sid Simon

- Sentence Prompt: Barbara Millis

- Snow Ball: Kari Fischer Uman and Jennifer Whitcomb

● PART ONE ●

. . . .

Setting the Stage

. . . .

CHAPTER ONE

· · · · · · · · ·

What Is a Team?

· ·

A rose may always be a rose, but a team is not always a team. So many groups are called teams these days that the word "team" has almost lost its meaning. There may be an "executive team," a "sales team," or even a "service team," but just calling a group a team does not make it so. There are certain criteria that a group must meet before it can be considered to be a team. As a way to determine whether a group is or is not a team, we have developed the classifications below.

● MODERN CLASSIFICATION OF TEAMS

Team Spirit Model

At one end of the spectrum is a group of people who are happy working for one boss, and everything seems to be going well. Some people might call it a team. In reality, these people have team spirit, but they are not a team because their boss calls all the shots. We call this the *Team Spirit Model*. They are not really a team because there is no sharing of authority or responsibility, which rests with the supervisor.

Cutting Edge Model

At the other end of the spectrum is a group of people who manage themselves. No one person in the group has the authority to make all the decisions about the events that impact the group. This group of people is referred to as a *self-directed* work team. And, indeed, they are a team because everyone has responsibility and authority for all the decisions they have to make. Some people call it a "leaderless" team. That name, however, creates an impression that no one is in charge. We call this the *Cutting Edge Model*.

Team Models

1. Team Spirit

2. Cutting Edge

3. Traditional

4. Task Force

5. Cyber Team

Traditional Model

In the middle between these extremes is a group of people who have a traditional boss, but who also share some of his or her responsibility and authority. How much is shared is usually dependent on the topic under discussion. A person is in charge; but on various issues, that person may allow other team members to take the leadership role. We call this the *Traditional Model*.

Task Force Model

In some cases, a group of people come together for a specific time to work on a special project or task. This grouping has traditionally been called a task force or a committee and includes "quality circles" as they are used in Total Quality Management (TQM) efforts and the "Workout Groups" popularized by General Electric in their quality effort. We call these groups the *Task Force Model*.

Cyber Teams

There is also a team model in which the members see one another infrequently or not at all. These teams are called "cyber" teams or "virtual" teams. What makes these teams different is that they have to work together to accomplish goal(s), but they may meet only at the beginning of their project and thereafter interact only through the use of the Internet and telephone. These cyber teams can fit any of the four models listed above in regard to controls and decision making. Cyber teams present a special challenge for training, as one cannot necessarily gather the members physically into one room.

Importance of Distinction

This distinction among types of teams is critical, because if you do not know the type of group you are working with, you may choose a game that is totally inappropriate. Depending on the type of group you are doing work with, you could be doing team training, team building, or just training in group dynamics. This distinction affects how you plan your work and what you expect as an outcome.

For example, say you are planning for the Traditional Model and prepare your training with that construct in mind. Then you find that the participants really fit into the Team Spirit Model, so everything you present on collaborative decision making and consensus building falls on deaf ears. Worse, your client may be upset that you are trying to change what he or she perceives as a good team. Obviously, knowing what type of team you will be working with is very important.

As you select any of the games in this book, keep in mind the type of team, how the team is structured, and whether the game is appropriate for the team model you are working with.

● DEFINITION OF A TEAM

We define a team as "A *group* of people who *come together,* under *shared leadership, mutual responsibility, and conscious authority,* to achieve *agreed-on goals* in a *mutually effective* fashion."

Group   The *group* that makes up a team usually consists of from three to eight people. If fewer than three, it is hard to say you even have a group. But if there are more than eight, you may have two teams, or at least a first and second string.

Who Come Together   A real team should be a group of people who *want* to work as a team. A group of people who are forced to be a team almost always create insurmountable problems. A task force, committee, quality circle, or workout group may not be a team because there may be members of the group who do not want to be there. They may be there because it would be "career limiting" not to be there. However, they do not contribute much energy or work to the group.

Shared Leadership   No one person is always in charge. Depending on the topic or situation, various team members share the leadership role. Just what that leadership role means in any situation is something that is determined differently by each type of team.

> *What Is a Team?*
>
> A *group* of people who *come together,* under *shared leadership, mutual responsibility, and conscious authority,* to achieve *agreed-on goals* in a *mutually effective* fashion.

Mutual Responsibility   The whole team is responsible for the work being accomplished. A good team does not assign work to one person and then forget about it. On a good team, if something is not being done, the whole team or members of the team take steps to ensure that the work is accomplished. A team that is mutually responsible does not blame individual members when a task is not accomplished. The whole team is aware of what must be done and by when.

Conscious Authority   The team thinks through how authority is going to be used by individual members and by the team leader. The team members make conscious decisions about how decisions will be made, how work will be assigned, how deadlines will be set, and about how the various tasks that face a team will be handled. Also, the team consciously sets working guidelines for itself.

Agreed-On Goals   The more freedom a team has in setting its own goals, the more it moves toward the Cutting Edge Model. If goals are imposed, then it is more in the Traditional Model. Agreement on goals is very important if a team is to fully utilize its energy. If people do not agree on a goal, it is doubtful that they will give it their full support. A member who strongly opposes a team goal may exhibit passive-aggressive behavior, saying he or she will do something and then not doing it. You and the rest of the group might find out about the non-agreement too late to correct the situation.

Even with agreed-on goals, conflict can develop over the distribution of resources and the methods and technology to be used to meet the goals. If goals are not agreed on, then an additional roadblock is added.

Mutually Effective   Being mutually effective means that the team does its work and that members have the appropriate skills to accomplish the tasks. There is a danger that a group of people may enjoy working together but still not accomplish the team tasks. This often happens in Rounds 2 or 3 of the RAT Race (page 151). A team is supposed to complete tasks. Teams are formed to do work, not just to have a good time. If work is not being done, then something is wrong.

Mutually effective also implies that everyone on the team has the skill level necessary to accomplish the tasks. If they do not have the appropriate skills, then the team itself must do something about developing those skills, through training or coaching. Members of a good team will not sit by and let a fellow team member flounder at his or her task. Both the team itself and the individual members must be successful in accomplishing their tasks.

Now that we have defined the different types of teams and what it means to be a team, we will explore how a team builds itself.

CHAPTER TWO

· · · · · · · · ·

Building a Team

· ·

An excellent description of team building comes from Richard Beckhard (1972). Beckhard said there are four activities that a group should perform on a regular basis if it desires to grow itself into a team:

1. Set and reset goals and priorities;

2. Analyze or allocate the way work is performed according to team members' roles and responsibilities;

3. Examine the way the team is working. What processes is the team using? Are they effective? How does the team cope with norms? What kind of decision making is the team engaged in? Where are communications effective? Does any aspect of the communication process need attention?; and

4. Examine how the group handles agreement, how it handles conflict, and how team members relate to one another around the task.

Activity One: Set and Reset Goals and Priorities

A group that is in the process of becoming a team must consciously determine its goals and their priority.

A rule of thumb: Whenever a conflict breaks out, have the participants try to state their goals. Many times, conflict happens either because there is confusion over the goals or because no one knows the goals. This is a phenomenon that you will encounter often as you use the games in this book. People will start the game without much attention to the goal for the game. Lack of attention to goals will lead to confusion in playing the game. As a facilitator, you will provide a great service to any team if you help the members learn the habit of being clear on goals before they start their work. However, you may have to let the team fail a couple of times on its own before the members are ready to learn that lesson.

The principle of "equifinality" (von Bertalanffy, 1968) says that there are many ways to reach the same goal in an open system. From the start of each game, there is going to be discussion on the best way to play. There will be very little discussion on the goals of the game. Imagine the conflict that will ensue when various methods are proposed and the goals are not clear. If the goals are clear, then at least you have some agreed-on yardstick to use to measure whether the proposed method will take you in the direction you want to go.

Not only must goals and priorities be set, but from time to time they must also be re-examined. First, if downsizing, restructuring, or re-engineering has impacted a team, team members need to reset priorities and goals. Yet many teams fail to do this. They may lose people or gain functions during downsizing, restructuring, or re-engineering, but they continue as if nothing has happened. Part of the reason may be because the announced goal of downsizing, restructuring, or re-engineering is often "to make the workforce more productive." People may feel as though they should not question the given goals or priorities. Of course, confusion results, but no one wants to address it. Here are two examples of teams that needed to re-examine their goals.

A certain municipal government organization suffered from a lack of clarity in goals. It was not politically expedient to admit that less service was going to be provided to citizens because of downsizing, so no re-examination of goals and priorities was done at the executive level; the front-line employees were left to make those decisions. The result was an increase in complaints from the citizens about certain services not being offered at the same level as before—just the type of complaint that the executives had hoped to avoid in their decision not to reset goals and priorities. The situation was frustrating to all the parties involved: the executives, the employees, and the citizens. Eventually some people lost their jobs because of this confusion over goals and priorities.

The second example is from a company that prints its yearly goals on 3" x 5" cards, laminates them, and gives them to each employee. As new ideas and suggestions are raised during the year, one of the first questions asked is, "How does that help us reach this year's goals?" People pull the cards out in meetings when confusion develops over the appropriateness of a certain action. To avoid stifling new ideas, the company created a committee that employees send their ideas to if the idea does not fit with the current year's goals. The ideas are then presented to the planning committee for inclusion into the following year's goals and objectives. This company pays attention to goals and priorities. As a result, most employees know how their performance is helping the organization achieve its goals.

The activities in this book that can help the team to focus *specifically* on goal setting are:

- Box of Chocolates
- Match Point
- RAT Race
- ww.where and ww.when

Activity Two: Analyze or Allocate the Way Work Is Performed According to Team Members' Roles and Responsibilities

Who does what is always a topic ripe for discussion. Many assumptions are likely to be made about what the other members are doing. This is especially true if there never has been a discussion about roles and responsibilities. Also, team tasks and responsibilities seem to change often, depending on the work required.

Of course, a Team Spirit Model team will not have much discussion because the supervisor makes these determinations. In the Traditional Model, depending on the amount of shared leadership, there may be a need for discussion. The danger with the Traditional Model is that the team members will let the supervisor determine responsibilities and then simply focus on their individual tasks.

For the Cutting Edge and Task Force Models, the team discussion of roles and responsibilities is of utmost importance, as no one is formally assigned the task of determining who does what. If the roles and responsibilities are not made explicit, chaos will reign and no work will be accomplished.

When roadblocks develop to accomplishing work, roles and responsibilities need to be revisited. Some team members may have been given too much work to accomplish. Other tasks may not have been assigned to anyone.

Many teams have found using a spreadsheet useful in this kind of situation. They list the team members' names down the side and the tasks and duties across the top of a page, then list the people who are primarily responsible for accomplishing tasks, who must be kept informed, who has decision-making authority, who will serve as a backup, and who has no involvement with the task.

Table 2.1. Sample Spreadsheet to Track Responsibility for Tasks

	Project Title	Budget	Phones	Customer	Supplies
Team Member					
Due Date		11-30-00	01-30-01	30th	1st
Sally		P	I	D	B
Jim		I	D	B	N
Reba		ID	B	N	D
Amid		D	P	ID	N
Renee		B	N	P	ID
Jason		N	ID	I	P

Legend:

P = Primary pesponsibility

I = Keep informed

D = Makes final decision

ID = Involved in decision-making process

B = Backup responsibility

N = Not involved

Table 2.1 is an example of this type of chart.

By reading this spreadsheet from time to time, the team members can assure themselves that important work will not be forgotten.

Another technique many teams use is to list under each task who does what with whom, when to start, and how the team knows when the task has been accomplished. This technique is very useful for reviewing task accomplishment. The list becomes both the team's action plan and evaluation tool. One caution: Some teams put in the phrase "as soon as possible" to identify when work should begin. That almost always ensures that nothing will be started. Other work will get in the way, so it never becomes "possible" to start the task. A specific date, such as Jan. 5, 2001, should always go in the "when" space. Table 2.2 is an example of this type of chart.

As you use the games contained in this book, you will find that it is productive to revisit Activity Two, "analyze or allocate the way work is performed according to

Table 2.2. Chart of Who Does What with Whom and When

Tasks	Purchase Computer	Create Marketing Plan	Create Projected Budget
Who	Sam and Barbara	Reba and Linda	Mariah and Nima
Does What	Purchase network system	Create artwork for marketing plan	Prepare draft budget for next year
With Whom	Purchasing	Printer Y	Sam, Barbara, Reba, and Linda
When to Start	March 1, 20XX	May 8, 20XX	Oct 1, 20XX
How Will We Know Project Is Finished	We are using a networked system by October 5, 20XX	Artwork will be on copy editor's desk by July 6, 20XX	Budget for next year is approved by Dec 1, 20XX

team members' roles and responsibilities," from time to time with the team. You may discover that two or three members of a team have taken on the same role, that some roles are left unfilled, or that some team members have assumed no role or responsibilities. By re-examining Activity Two, these problems can be found and corrected.

Teams often will begin to play a game with no discussion of roles and responsibilities, letting them evolve as they move along. When roles and responsibilities are not discussed at the beginning, the resulting confusion becomes one of the reasons the team members give to explain why they didn't accomplish the task well.

To avoid this natural tendency to not be clear on roles and responsibilities, some facilitators bring it to the team's attention before starting to play a game. Even if a team does discuss roles and responsibilities at the beginning, it needs to discuss them again as the game progresses, as certain realities develop that were not evident earlier. Here is an example of what happened during one team training situation.

One of the simulation exercises on survival was being used. One of the team members proposed that he should be the team leader because he had attended survival training and had been a Green Beret in the jungles of Vietnam. Initially, the rest of the team went along with this decision. During the consensus-seeking discussion, a much older man in the group kept trying to suggest a different ranking for some of the items. The elected team leader went out of his way to tell the older man why he was wrong.

When the scoring was done, the Green Beret's group had the worst team score. The older man had the best individual score in the room. It seemed that he and his sons sometimes spent weekends in the mountains with just a quart of water and a sleeping bag each. They lived off the land for an entire weekend. His experience was actually more pertinent to the group task than the former Green Beret's experience.

As a result of this experience, this team became much more conscious of how roles and responsibilities were assigned for the rest of the workshop.

The same phenomenon can happen with a work team. At the beginning, it is all discussion. Once work begins, the group can see who has what skills. Rearranging roles and responsibilities is not uncommon once a team actually begins to work. There is a need to discuss roles and responsibilities on a regular basis. The most pertinent game in this book for addressing these issues is RAT Race.

Activity Three: Examine the Way the Team Is Working

What processes does the team use? Are they effective? How does the team cope with norms? What kind of decision making is the team engaged in? Where are communications effective? Where do they need some work?

Various practices develop as a team goes about its work. As with other things that grow naturally, "weeds" in the form of poor habits and procedures can crop up and get in the way. A team may not notice unless it takes the time to look at how it works together. A procedure or process may have been instituted that was valid at one time, but is no longer useful. A team could keep performing this process unless it takes time to examine all of its processes and their consequences. Here's an example of this situation.

A team held one team meeting a week. One of the complaints that always came up was that various team members felt "out of the loop." The team meetings themselves were good, but during the interval between meetings some things happened that some members were totally unaware of—even though they had been at the most recent meeting.

Upon examining their processes, with the help of a third party, the team decided that one meeting a week was not enough to keep everyone informed, so the team set up a major meeting once a week with smaller stand-up meetings every morning in which everyone would be brought up-to-date. The result was a smoother functioning team. If this team had not examined its processes, the members would not have discovered that at least one of them needed to be changed.

Another example of Activity Three was a team that had decided that on major issues, such as budget, equipment, staffing levels, and new projects, everyone had to (1) be at the meeting, (2) read the necessary documentation, (3) state the reasons behind their thinking, and (4) vote. These four steps seemed to work for a while.

Luckily, because this team took time out every quarter to look at how it was working, members noticed that a lot of decisions were being put off because people were not coming to the meetings prepared. They discovered that some team members were not reading the necessary documentation; were not requesting extra time prior to the meeting; and were asking for a postponement at the meetings. So the team made an auxiliary rule: "If you have not read the material, and you have not asked for a postponement before the meeting, you cannot vote on the issue under consideration." This rule had an impact, especially the first time someone could not vote on his own budget because he had not read the budget projections.

The next time this team looked at its decision-making process it noticed that there were very few decisions being postponed. If the team had not taken the time to re-examine its process, it might still be delaying decisions and falling behind on task accomplishment.

Paying attention to process is very important for improving the performance of a team. However, paying attention to process is not a skill that is taught in the school system. The participants will learn how to pay attention to process by watching you, the facilitator, pay attention to process.

You will notice that some of the activities in this book do not have a means to declare who wins and who loses. You will also notice that some of the activities do not focus on content that is directly related to team building. The reason is that in building a team, process is content. The quality of a team's process is directly related to the quality of a team's productivity. So some activities just focus on a team's process, rather than on content, because process is so important.

It is debatable how much a facilitator can help a team with its actual work. The facilitator's primary focus should be on the *process* the team uses in doing that work. Improve the process, improve the work.

A team must also analyze how it communicates. Is everyone receiving the necessary information? Is the information useful? Is there information a team is not receiving that it needs? Are the team's meetings effective? Does the team have too many or too few meetings? Do team members take time to listen to one another, or do they assume that listening has occurred? These questions need to be answered by every team.

You can be certain that a team's natural behaviors will be displayed when it plays the games in this book. If a team's communication process creates problems while the members are playing the games, you will know that the communication process causes problems while the members are accomplishing its tasks. Help the team find new behaviors to play the game successfully, and they can use those new behaviors back at work. To help the team focus, ask, "What occurs at work when your communication process breaks down the way it did here?" If the team wants to improve and the behavior is discussable, members will tell you what happens. You can then offer the team a chance to try new behaviors as it replays the game or plays a different one. In this way, team members practice new behaviors before they have to use them.

Team Norms

Norms are unwritten rules that team members follow, but do not discuss. Have you ever been to a meeting with a new group and said something that produced absolute silence in the room? You can be assured that you probably just touched on a norm of the group. You wanted to discuss something that was not discussable. After the meeting, you were probably filled in on why that topic is not discussed. Norms can get in the way of a team accomplishing its task, and they are hard to address. Not only are some norms not discussable, but the fact that they cannot be discussed is not discussable either. If team members do want to discuss their norms, they probably need a person from outside the team to help them with the process. If in the process of playing the games in this book with teams, you find that a team will not discuss certain issues, you have probably uncovered a norm.

Your best approach in this case is to ask team members what the consequences are of not discussing what has occurred. Ask what happens to task accomplishment because this behavior is not discussed; what price the team pays for not discussing this norm; and what will happen if the team does discuss this norm. Ask who they think will be hurt and how.

Decision Making

How does a team handle making decisions? Has there been open discussion of how decisions will be made? Will the same method be used for every decision?

It is probably not necessary for any team to decide everything with the same decision-making style. Yet the common thinking seems to be that all team decisions should be made by consensus. There are those who mistake consensus decision making with unanimity.

Consensus means that the participants are willing to support the decision that has been made. Consensus does not mean that support should be construed as 100 percent agreement with the decision. *Unanimity means that everyone has 100 percent agreement and support of the decision.* When was the last time that happened?

Support is the most important point. Once a decision has been made, energy must be expended to implement it. If someone cannot lend 100 percent support, then that person's energy will be lost during the implementation stage.

If the decision only affects one or two people on the team, there is probably no need to have the whole team involved in the decision-making process. Perhaps the people who make the decision can just report it back to the team as a piece of information.

The games in this book that can help the team focus *specifically* on the issues under decision making are:

- Bell Hop
- Box of Chocolates
- Duel Identity
- Norman Says!
- RAT Race
- Regards
- Super Model

Activity Four: Examine How the Group Handles Agreement, How It Handles Conflict, and How Team Members Relate to One Another Around the Task

Most people do not see agreement as a problem. They say, "Well, isn't agreement what we are after in the first place?" Agreement is not a problem, if it is actually agreement.

Silence is often misinterpreted as agreement. Remember that the only place silence means consent is in a court of law. In team building, silence can usually be interpreted as indicating that someone has reservations, but is not willing to speak up.

Jerry Harvey (1988) has brilliantly illustrated in *The Abilene Paradox* that people may be too polite to bring up objections to a plan. Silence can also mean that people do not care, that they want to make a decision and get it over with. These people are not likely to raise any issue that would slow down the decision-making process. In extreme cases, there may be people who remain silent because they want to see the decision fail. In this case, one could question whether the team is really a team.

How does one check to see whether silence really is agreement? Here are two helpful techniques:

1. The first is to go around the team and have everyone complete the following sentence: "I support the decision to [state just what it is they agree to support]." People with major reservations cannot complete the sentence, and their reservations can be expressed.

2. The second technique is to put the decision aside for awhile and come back to it at a later date with any reservations. Ask the whole team to act as devil's advocates. In the devil's advocate meeting, all members have to state what is wrong with the decision, either verbally or on Post-it® Notes that are hung on the wall and grouped according to theme. The group can then address the issues.

You may not want to use these techniques for all decisions, as both methods do take extra time. However, when major decisions face a team, the techniques are valuable to make sure that support is there for the decision.

Conflict

The next issue a team has to face is how it handles conflict. There is a misperception that a team that has conflict has something wrong. Conflict should not be viewed as either good or bad. It is just something that happens between humans when they interact. Conflict comes to every relationship sooner or later. Seeing conflict as neutral and inevitable goes a long way toward helping to resolve it.

Studies have shown that the highest level of conflict occurs among high performers. This is probably because they are all sure they are right! So a high-performing team can be assured that conflict will be present as team members interact with one another. The issue is not whether or not conflict occurs. Rather, the issue is how the team manages the conflict that does occur.

In any model of team development, there is a conflict stage. Unless a team learns how to manage its conflict, it will never become a productive problem-solving entity. If conflict is suppressed, then the team will never become a team and the group will remain relatively passive, doing only what it is told to do. And the telling has to be rather specific and detailed.

Teams must learn how to manage conflict. They must develop guidelines for how conflict will be surfaced, how it will be managed, and how each team member can help solve it. In no instance should conflict be seen as a problem with the team leader's level of skill in leading a team—the members are jointly responsible for solving it.

One way to begin to solve conflict is for team members to learn how to state their concerns openly. Until all members share what is troubling them, it is not possible to solve a conflict. When conflict occurs, have team members complete the following sentence, "What concerns me about this [issue, decision, etc.] is. . . ." If some members of the team do not feel that they are involved in the conflict, they may serve as third-party moderators.

After all concerns are out in the open, then the team can address them. Once the conflict has been solved, the team can review how it solved the conflict and develop operating guidelines for managing the next conflict.

The activities in this book that can help a team to focus *specifically* on conflict issues are:

- Cross Roads
- Duel Identity
- Line Up
- Power Tag
- Sentence Prompt
- Tooth and Nail

Up to now we have discussed what a team is and how to build a team. In the next chapter we will look more closely at the role of the facilitator. The quality of the facilitation a team receives is critical in helping a team to build itself.

References

Beckhard, R. (1972). Optimizing team-building efforts. *Journal of Contemporary Business, 1*(3): 23–32.

Harvey, J.B. (1988). *The Abilene paradox and other meditations on management.* San Francisco, CA: Jossey-Bass/Pfeiffer.

von Bertalanffy, L. (1968). *General system theory.* New York: George Braziller.

CHAPTER THREE

· · · · · · · ·

Facilitation

· ·

Sally waits for her students to arrive for her team-building course. She is more prepared than she was last time. She has done more research and has substantially
improved her lecture on team building. Sally has even produced a PowerPoint®
presentation for one segment. This course will certainly be better than the last
course she taught on team building. Her lecture has been improved, and she has a
game to play after lunch.

The last time Sally taught the course, the group's energy level was low the entire
time, despite her good overheads. The energy level really went down after lunch
that time, so Sally has found a good game on goal setting that she is going to use
after lunch. She has lengthened her presentation on goal setting in the morning so
that the audience will be well-prepared for the game after lunch. Goal setting is
very important for a team. This game should really drive that point home.

The morning presentation goes no better than the last time. For some reason the
participants just do not seem to get too excited about Sally's presentation. The
material is so important, and she cannot understand their lack of enthusiasm. Well,
it will be different after lunch.

After lunch Sally introduces the game to the participants, who seem pretty
enthused about it. She explains the rules and procedures and divides the class into
groups. They are ready to play.

As the game progresses, Sally notices that the teams are just not getting it. Not one
team has mentioned the concept of goals. Don't they remember that from her lecture this morning? After two rounds she stops the game and reviews her lecture on

goals with them. Now they remember. She tells them that before they play the next round they need to focus on the goals and objectives for the game.

So the teams set their goals, play the game, and achieve better results. However, the teams do not seem very energetic. The debriefing of the game results in no new learning for the participants. They just repeat back what Sally has told them twice.

When the class is over, Sally is disappointed by the ratings she receives and does not know why the course has gone no better than the first time, despite all her extra effort. Maybe the participants just did not want to be there in the first place. Maybe they just didn't care.

Meanwhile, on the Other Side of Town . . .

The office staff has to get up and once again close the door on Linda's classroom. There is just too much noise coming out of that room. They talk among themselves as to what kind of class Linda is teaching. How could she be teaching a class on team building with all that noise in the room?

When the evaluations are turned in, the participants give Linda very high marks for the course. A few participants even come into the office to say what a wonderful class they have been in and that Linda has taught them a lot about teams. The participants say they really loved the games that Linda has played with them all day.

"Games?" the office staff wonders. Linda was supposed to be teaching a class, not playing games. Maybe that's why there is no problem in filling up Linda's classes; she plays games rather than teaching. So they decide that someone will sit in on the next class Linda teaches to see whether she is really teaching a course on team building.

A senior trainer sits in on Linda's next class. He is amazed at how Linda teaches the class. She never lectures for more than five minutes at a time. She keeps the students moving around with the various games she plays with them. And do the students ever have questions! And they engage in animated discussion with one another. They surely seem to be learning about teams.

Linda seems to be more of an activity director than a trainer. She proposes a game, explains the rules, and lets the participants go. Between rounds Linda asks questions that seem to help the participants to reflect on their behavior, the consequences of that behavior, and options for future behavior. Then, after each game, Linda asks the participants to write a paper on how they could use what they have learned back on the job. The participants then share what they have written with one another.

The senior trainer reports back to the staff the next day. "Well," he says, "Linda sure is unconventional. I wouldn't call what she does training, but there is no doubt that the students were learning. And they were learning a lot that they could use back at work. Maybe we had better talk to Linda and find out what she calls what she does. It sure works."

● DEFINITION OF FACILITATION

What Linda does is called facilitation for adult learners. Facilitation provides people an opportunity to learn about their behavior. And participants learn in a way that is more lasting than listening to a lecture. Adults would rather discover meaningful knowledge for themselves than listen to what someone else thinks is important.

Remember the bromide that says that people remember more of what they do than what they see or hear? Facilitation is based on that premise. If people do something that they learn from, they will remember it longer than if they just hear or see it.

Facilitation increases the ease with which any action is performed by the continued successive application of the necessary stimulus. This book provides twenty-one games or activities to stimulate learning. The challenge of the game itself and the questions asked by the facilitator stimulate learning.

By doing something over and over again, people learn how to behave in a new way. Resistance is lessened through practicing new behavior. As a result people have an easier time using new behaviors when they go back to work.

● STYLES OF FACILITATION

People's facilitation style is dependant on how they view their role in adult learning. People who like to be the "Sage on Stage" tend to be very directive. They may use a game to drive home a point. They will push and shape the group to learn the lesson they want it to learn. If any other issue comes up from the audience, they will either not deal with it until later, treat it in a summary fashion, or ignore it.

Many facilitators run into difficulty by trying to force the participants to learn what they want them to learn. For example, let's say that during the course of playing a game that deals with problem solving, one of the participants tells the class that playing games is a waste of time and just for children.

A Sage on Stage will tell the offender why he or she is wrong. The Sage will tell the participants what the game has to offer in helping them solve problems, that the course is about problem solving, and that this game is part of the course. The Sage will tend to put down the protestor and thereby shut the door on future protests by the participants. The Sage will thus have eliminated any opportunity group members have to internalize the lessons that perhaps need to be learned.

At the other end of the spectrum is the facilitator who is more Socratic in practice. Commonly called a process facilitator, this person is aware of the principles of adult learning and realizes that "readiness to learn" (Knowles, 1980, p. 44) is more crucial to real learning than the lesson plan. The process facilitator focuses on the learning available in the moment, rather than the learning called for by the course outline.

Let's look at a problem participant through the eyes of a process facilitator. First, a process facilitator will fully explore why the participant is upset, ask why the participant feels as he or she does about the game, and ask for alternatives from the participant's point of view. The process facilitator gives the problem participant plenty of time to explain his or her viewpoint and how it was formed.

Then, seizing this teachable moment, the facilitator might ask the participants to write what they would do in a situation that is not working out as planned. The Socratic facilitator would work with the participants to come up with alternative behaviors that might turn the situation around and thus turn a possible confrontation into a learning event.

● THE BEGINNING

Most adults want to know something about what they are going to be doing, so the beginning of the game is critical to the process. As a facilitator, it is important to explain to the participants *what* they are going to be doing; the *why* should only be explained in very global terms.

You want the participants to play the game using the same natural, unreflective behaviors that they would use at work. If you provide an extensive explanation of the game, then the participants may use behaviors that will help them with the game, but that they would not use back at work. You want them to see the results that their natural behaviors produce—to assure them that their behaviors are productive or give them solid reasons for changing their behaviors.

At the beginning of the game, state the goal in global terms at the macro level. If the game is on goal setting, you might say something like, "This game will help us look at how we organize work. Everyone has more work to do than time to do it. This game will help us find answers to that problem."

Go on to explain the rules of the game and how the game will proceed. In a game that is played in rounds, let the participants know that you will be asking some questions between the rounds. In a game with continuous play, let them know that you may stop the game from time to time to ask some questions.

After you have explained the rules of the game, the participants are in their appropriate work groups, and they have the materials they need, then start the play.

From time to time you will have people who let it be known that they have no desire to play games. In that case you can make them observers of the process to keep them involved in a constructive manner. Assign them the task of keeping track of the process each group is using. To help them do that, it is good policy to have some observer sheets for them to fill out. Once the processing stage begins, the observers can participate by sharing with the group what they have observed. For all practical purposes they become your assistants.

● DURING PLAY

Once play begins, your role is to make sure the rules are being followed and to observe the process each group is using. Once the process begins to unfold, become attuned to what is happening in the groups and respond appropriately to each situation as it arises. Because the learning is now participant driven, it becomes almost impossible to explain each situation that may arise. Some guidelines that you may find useful are presented below.

Interpreting Rules

When you are asked to interpret a rule, and there is no firm definition of what the rule means, let the group members interpret it for themselves.

For example, say the rule says that "The group must decide the best response to A." You might be asked whether that decision must be by majority vote, consensus, unanimous, etc. Appropriate responses to that question are either: "You decide" or "What would be the best style for the situation?" Don't give the group an answer. What is under investigation is their own ideas, so do not put yourself into the group.

If, on the other hand, the rules say only one person may speak at a time and the group asks if two people can speak, the answer is obviously no. The rules are clear on that.

If the rules do not speak to what the group asks you, the appropriate response is again to tell the group to decide. It is the members' behavior that is under study, not your interpretation.

Handling Complaints

When someone complains about something, the best question to ask is, "What would you like to do or change?" The purpose is to help participants to be proactive about their participation in the total experience. Avoid, if possible, explaining why something has been done. Focus on what the participants did and why. Focus on what the participants would like to change and why. This will give them a sense of ownership and empowerment—two concepts that can translate back to the workplace.

Dealing with Blame

You may notice that unsuccessful teams blame you for their failure. A team may even start to blame other teams for its failure. The blame usually sounds like:

- The other team cheated because they had more players.

- The words in the game are wrong, biased in some fashion.

- The game has nothing to do with the topic we are studying.

This is called *perceptual defense* or *self-serving bias,* the tendency for people to protect themselves against ideas, objects, or situations that are threatening to their own self-image. The participants are finding their failure troublesome and probably threatening to their own sense of competency. Therefore, to make the situation less threatening, the participants begin to blame others outside of the team.

Another way the participants try to protect themselves is by withdrawing from the game. They become very passive. Their thinking is that if they do not participate they cannot be held responsible for the results.

A self-serving bias is the tendency of people to accept responsibility for good performance but to deny responsibility for poor performance. This is most often seen during performance appraisal time. A person wants to be rewarded for things that have gone well, but will go to great lengths to explain why something that went poorly was beyond his or her control.

The participants will blame external factors for their own poor performance. What they do not see is that they are attributing a certain motivation to the people they are blaming, while not accepting their own responsibility for their lack of success.

Managing Disagreements

Sometimes disagreement can keep the team from accomplishing its goals in the game. Here is a procedure to follow when disagreement begins over such things as interpretation of the rules, meaning of a task, or what is to be learned from the games.

1. Establish agreement about just what was said, done, felt, or thought. Any discussion or dialogue will fail until there is agreement on what took place and the meaning of any written directions.

2. Separate facts, which everyone can agree on, from assumptions and interpretations, which may be open to widely different views.

3. Keep asking the participants *why* they say what they do or think what they think. Do not let them get away with an answer such as, "It just is," "That is how we have to do it," or any other answer that does not include the "why." Uncover the assumptions under their behavior or comments. Then question whether those assumptions are valid. If you cannot explain why you say or do something, but believe it to be right, then more than likely it has been programmed into you at some point by others. It is exactly this pre-programmed, unexamined assumption that leads us into doing or saying things that are unproductive.

4. Agree on the learning that took place. Based on that learning, develop agreed-on procedures for continuing. If you use a new method, you should be able to state the hypothesis you are going to test with that new method.

5. Try the new method and see what happens. Does it prove the hypothesis? Were you more effective on task accomplishment? What effect did the new method have on relationships in the group?

Dealing with Resistance

If resistance develops during play of a game, you have a fertile opportunity to discuss resistance to change and how to overcome it. You could ask what it would take for the participants to want to continue with the game, what is it they do not understand, what would have to change, and so on. Once you have overcome their resistance, you can ask why they are now willing to continue.

You can come back to this experience of resistance at the end of the game and ask what they have learned about overcoming resistance to change and how what they learned could be used when implementing any changes they are trying to make on the job.

If play becomes bogged down during the game, here are some questions you can ask to get the group to look its process.

1. What is happening?

2. What do you want to happen?

3. What behaviors are producing the results you say you do not want?

4. Can you substitute new behaviors for any of the behaviors that are not working and get better results?

5. What would you do in any setting outside the classroom if this were occurring? Do you want to do that here?

6. Can you do this in another way?

7. Could you offer a suggestion to get the game back on track?

8. What would you prefer?

    a. What results might that produce?

    b. Do you want those results?

Ending Game Play

When to end the play of a game can be difficult to decide. If the purpose of playing a game is to produce learning in or elicit learning from the team, then do not end the game until the learning has occurred.

We have listed a range of time it will take to play some of the games in this book because it is impossible to know how long it will take for learning to occur. Never feel bound by the suggested time, which is given only as a guideline. Do not let a guideline get in the way of learning. Do not end a game simply because the guidelines say that the game should take one hour.

An easy way to know when the learning is over is to pay attention to the energy level of the team. If the energy level is high, as evidenced by lively discussion and interaction, then facilitate the learning that is occurring. If you sense that the energy level is low, then that is probably the appropriate time to end the game.

● AFTER PLAY

Your role now is to help the participants discover the learning from what they have done—not to put your learning on them. You may clearly see what lessons they have learned well and what lessons still need some work. That's good, but your task is not to tell them, but—through a series of questions—to help them to see the lesson themselves. Remember that the lesson they need to learn may not be the lesson you want to teach.

For example, we divided a large group into teams to play RAT Race. The teams had the clear choice of working together to achieve their goals or for each team to play on its own. Every team chose to proceed on its own. Needless to say, none of the teams did well. When it came time to process the game, we wanted to look at what behaviors helped and what behaviors hindered the achievement of the goal. What the participants wanted to talk about was why they chose to be competitive. Their biggest complaint was that they could not be effective supervisors because their peers and managers were so competitive and did not want to share. What they discovered was that they were no different from the people they were complaining about. They saw that, although the class contained only peers, they had still chosen to be competitive rather than cooperative. This was a big eyeopener to the participants, and we spent three hours talking about why people want to be competitive rather than cooperative and what could be done.

Although the topic we talked about was of great use to those teams, it was not the topic we originally had in mind. If we had continued to push our own agenda, then the teams would never have experienced the learning that they did.

Once you start a game, you never know for sure exactly where it is going to end up. You cannot know ahead of time what lessons will be learned. You can have a working hypothesis about what lessons might be learned; however, you need to be flexible enough to allow the natural lessons to occur.

Your role as facilitator is to help participants develop their own insights into what happened and to help them to turn those insights into some learning. You need a certain element of trust that the process will unfold in a direction useful to the group.

Each group has its own lessons to learn. So the lessons learned by one set of groups may not be the same lessons learned by another set of groups. You should not try to force the same learning for each group you work with. Help each group to develop the insights that are meaningful to the members.

Establishing Reality

The first part of processing should be establishing what did happen. This can be difficult if there is not general agreement about what occurred. The questions below can be used to help everyone come to agreement about what occurred during the play of the game. Remember that you are not interpreting what happened, but only trying to figure out what happened. While you are gathering the group's answers to these questions, it is advisable to write the answers on a flip chart yourself or with the help of one of the observers.

1. What happened?

   a. Who did what?

   b. Who said what?

   c. What were the results?

2. What are you surprised about? Was anyone surprised about something different?

3. Are you in a quandary about anything?

4. How do you feel about what happened?

   a. Does anyone feel differently?

   b. Does everyone feel the same way?

5. Was the stated objective achieved or not?

Establishing Meaning

You are now ready to begin looking at the meaning of what occurred. The objective at this stage is to come to some common agreement as to how to interpret what occurred. For this, you can use the following questions:

1. What does what happened mean for you?

   a. Does anyone have other meanings?

   b. Does anyone disagree with the meanings?

2. Why do you think that event occurred?

3. Do you see a consistent pattern of behavior?

4. What does what happened suggest to you about the group? About yourself?

5. Is there a pattern behind the data we have agreed on?

6. Does what happened here happen at work also?

   a. If not, why not?

   b. If not, how do you account for the difference in behavior?

7. Do you see some underlying principle(s) in operation here?

8. Have you had this experience before? If so, where, when, and under what circumstances?

9. How do you feel about [accomplishing/not accomplishing] the goals of the game?

Applying the Learning

Now that you have determined the facts of the matter and what they mean, you are ready to lead the participants in a discussion on how they will apply their learning back at work. The application phase is the main reason you play games in the first place—to derive meaning through observation of behavior that will lead to a change in workplace behavior.

At this point, you want the participants to decide ways to apply the lessons they have learned back at work and how they will make use of their learning. Here are some questions you might ask:

1. Because of this experience what might you do differently back at work?

2. What have you learned from this experience?

   a. Have you learned that lesson before?

   b. If so, what do you think will make the lesson stick so that you do not have to learn it again?

3. Because of this experience what might you *continue* doing back at work?

4. Because of this experience what might you *stop* doing back at work?

5. Because of this experience what might you *start* doing back at work?

6. A year from now, what do you hope will be different because of what you have learned from playing this game?

7. What might help you do different things back at work?

8. Whose help would you need to implement these changes?

9. How do you hinder yourself in this type of situation at work?

10. Based on what you have learned, how could you help yourself now?

11. What would be the hardest new thing for you to try at work? Why would that be difficult?

12. What could you imagine happening at work if you tried these new behaviors?

● FEEDBACK PHASE

Now that you have spent time discussing the participants' behavior during the game, it is time for them to look at yours. Allowing the participants to give you feedback helps solidify the learning bond between them and you. It shows that you are willing to "walk the talk." Some questions you can use to solicit feedback follow:

1. If I were to use this game again, what changes would you suggest in how the game is played?

2. What is there about how the game was presented that should be repeated next time?

3. What is there about the game itself that should be changed or eliminated for the next time?

4. What was the best part of this game?

5. Was the learning you obtained from playing the game worth the effort to play the game?

● SALLY OR LINDA

You have the choice of how to present the games in this book. You can be like Sally, the Sage on Stage, or you can be like Linda, the Socratic Facilitator. The choice is yours. And you will get the same results they did.

In this chapter you have been exposed to the various roles you can play as a facilitator of team-building games. You have been supplied with questions that can help you harvest learning from them.

In the next chapter, we walk you through the steps and procedures for playing the games and introduce you to a seven-step model that can be used for any game you decide to play.

Reference

Knowles, M.S. (1980). *The modern practice of adult education.* Chicago, IL: Follett.

CHAPTER FOUR

· · · · · · · ·

Team Games

· ·

The culture of an organization shows up in its play.

George Takacs

Games create an interactive learning experience by transforming participants into active players and translating inactive information into playful learning episodes.

By participating in a team game, the team undergoes a shared experience—a reality that can be observed, acknowledged, and discussed. Because every team brings its own set of experiences and history to the training, you have to place the team in an experience that is structured and controlled. The team members can then reflect back on this event and learn from it, building from this shared moment.

Twenty-one shared learning experiences are included in this book. Many of the games offer more than one learning opportunity. For example, in the RAT Race game, the initial focus is problem solving. After two rounds, the issue shifts to feedback and goal setting. And, as play continues into the third and fourth round, players find that team learning itself becomes an important issue. Many of these team games force players to look not only at themselves but at the box in which they play. This is a team learning moment that would be hard to replicate with any lecture.

The games featured in this book underscore many of the skills that make teams effective, specifically problem solving, team communication, creativity, conflict management, team learning, leadership and authority, decision making, goal setting, norms, feedback, meeting management, planning, trust, and cooperation.

These skills are not directly taught, but rather become part of behaviors that surface during game play. Once acknowledged, they become part of the post-game debriefing.

● GAME FORMAT

Each game in this book is formatted for easy review, set-up, and play. The features of each game are highlighted to allow you to browse, then use what you want. Each game begins with information about possible applications and ends with tips on customizing the game for your own audience.

The following information is given for each game:

- *Purpose:* The skills and applications covered in the game, as shown in the matrix of teaching skills and team types reflected in the Book at a Glance grid on page 47.

- *Time:* The minimum time one should devote to playing this particular game. Additional time may be needed for a debriefing.

- *Players:* The recommended number of players for playing the game. For larger groups, you may want to create several subgroups of approximately the recommended number.

- *Supplies:* The resources needed to set up and play the game. Most of the resources are easily obtained from home or office supply cupboards.

- *Steps:* Gives each step in playing the game.

- *Sample Round of Play or Scoring:* Included as needed, to demonstrate the flow of the game or to provide a solution, as with Cross Roads and Line Up.

- *Facilitator Notes:* Provides additional insight for the facilitator. This unique feature provides questions, insights, background, applications, resources, and concepts for use and application of the game.

- *Customizing:* Gives additional ideas of how to adapt the game in terms of group size, time, focus of the task, and scoring.

- *Player Instructions:* Provides a reproducible set of game rules so that you can post them during play, eliminating many questions from the team.

- *Materials:* Reproducible game sheets, game cards, inventories, reference sheets, score sheets, sample commentary, and other materials needed for each specific game.

● PREPARE AND PLAY: A SEVEN-STEP MODEL

Use the model below as a guide and review for any of the games in the book. It will serve as a reminder of the planning steps in finding, setting up, playing, and debriefing your own game.

To help you put this model to immediate use, we have taken one of the games from the book, Cross Roads (pages 83–90), and used the model on it. Of course, after conducting any game you may want to make notes on what worked and what should be changed the next time you use it.

Step 1. Game Selection: Cross Roads

Target Audience

The most important consideration is your audience. Your game must reflect their knowledge, skills, abilities, and work environments.

Level of Play: Teams   Here you determine your audience's intellectual level and game experience and their expectations for quality of rules and the depth of questions they may ask.

Length of Game: Fifty Minutes or More   Decide how long the game should take. You may wish to allow additional time for Cross Roads, such as fifteen minutes for set-up and twenty-five minutes for the debriefing.

Number of Players: Eight or More   List the total number of active participants or, in the case for Cross Roads, four players on each team. Other participants may be assigned roles as observers and judges.

Learning Outcomes

The learning outcomes for Cross Roads are team communication, team problem solving and memory, inter-team conflict, and how to think "outside of the box." You will want to list yours here.

Game Features

Every game has its own format, a pattern of play, and rules. A suitable game should have a mix of simplicity and challenge. Cross Roads features the following:

- *Floor Game:* Game is played on a road made on the floor.

- *Physical Involvement:* Game uses eight players as "pawns" and other players as observers.

- *Continuing Play:* Game can be played in one round or broken up into planning and playing rounds.

- *Simple Format:* Although easy to learn, game play can be very challenging, sometimes frustrating.

- *Team Planning:* Game requires team to understand overall game objective, as well as how to move on game paths.

- *Real-Time Communication:* Game play requires continuous communication between the player "pawns."

Customizing

Each game includes a section to allow you to adapt it for use with a particular group or to accommodate a specific time frame. Cross Roads can be varied regarding group size, time, and focus of the task.

Regarding Group Size This game can be adapted for groups of four players ranging from four to sixteen. Additional players can be assigned roles as observers and recorders. For much larger groups you may wish to create additional subgroups and run several games.

Regarding Time Shorten or expand time of play, as necessary. Also, allow additional time for teams to hold planning meetings.

Regarding Focus of the Task Set up the game for twelve players by placing additional spaces on floor. You may also add additional players to act as "floor supervisors" to counsel active players during game play or conduct team meetings.

Step 2: Game Content

Demonstration of Learning

A game presents an opportunity to place information before a newly motivated participant. Use your introductory lecture, post-game debriefing, handout materials, and take-home information for this purpose. For Cross Roads we suggest materials on creative thinking, thinking "outside the box," or other intuitive/right-brain approaches to problem solving.

Developing Debriefing Materials

You may want to develop a checklist of questions to lead your team through the debriefing. Experience will guide you for which questions to use and when, but having a list ready will help guide you through the game your first time. Here are some questions you might want to ask during the play of Cross Roads:

- What are you doing?
- Is it working?
- What might you do differently?

Step 3: Game Accessories

Cross Roads is a floor game that requires eight players to move across two "roads" of spaces constructed of newspaper sections or made of masking tape. Here is a list of materials and accessories that will help you set up and conduct the game.

Game Materials

- *Newspapers:* To create a game arena you need nine squares, representing a crossing road, made up of sections of newspapers or cardboard placed on the floor.

- *Masking Tape:* Use this to tape down newspaper sections or to create the "spaces" of the road, as well as to place charts or information on walls.

- *Felt-Tipped Markers:* You will need several markers for a variety of tasks, from filling out name cards to listing responses on a flip chart.

Audiovisual Equipment

- *Flip Chart:* Use to list points from a lecture, display game objectives and rules of play, and list comments and reactions.

- *Overhead Projector:* Display the Player Instructions, helpful lecture material, and comments and reactions.

- *Audiotape Player:* Play background music and introduce audio information from speeches or soundtracks. (If you choose to use music or other pre-recorded audiotapes, be sure to observe copyright regulations.)

Special Props and Accessories

- *Stopwatch:* Time game play, team meetings, or debriefing.

- *Noisemaker:* Use as a playful way to alert teams to start and stop play. A noise-maker can also be used to remind participants when to return from break.

- *Name Cards/Tent Folds:* Create an informal networking environment or use to assign roles and allow teams to create team names.

Step 4: Pre-Game Set-Up

Take this time to walk through your game as you set up your game environment.

Game Set-Up

Make sure you have enough room to lay out nine squares of newspaper (or tape), with additional areas for observation and team meetings.

1. Lay out one row of five square spaces, with 12 to 18 inches between them.

2. Place two road spaces outward from the middle space to form a perpendicular intersection, as shown below.

Suggested Game Layout

3. Set up conference tables, chairs, and name cards.

4. Post rules of play and other materials.

5. Set up instructor's table with handouts, reference materials, transparencies, and miscellaneous supplies needed for the game.

Step 5: Game Preliminaries

Preliminaries are the in-class procedures prior to actual game play that help create the structure and environment of the game.

Display Game Information

- Show game objective and Player Instructions on overhead.

Player Instructions for Cross Roads

- Select two sets of four players.
- Each player stands on one space, facing center, leaving the center space open.
- Players must cross to the other side of the road.

Legal Moves

- A player may move into an empty space in front of him or her.
- A player may move around someone facing him or her into an empty space.
- Only one player may move at a time.

Illegal Moves

- A player may not move backward.
- A player may not move around someone facing the same way.
- Two players may not move at the same time.
- Two players cannot occupy the same space.
- No player may step off of the game space.

Introduce the Game

Your introduction should both introduce the game and motivate learners to play. Here's a sample introduction for Cross Roads.

"Good morning, I want to briefly go over the game, Cross Roads. This is a floor game, during which players move on a "road" constructed from newspaper or masking tape squares. One player stands on each space, leaving the center space free. The object of the game is to successfully move all your team's players to the other side of the road. The Player Instructions are posted on the overhead. [You may wish to go over the Player Instructions, shown above, with the group.] The game is over when all players have successfully crossed to the other side of the road."

Conduct Warm-Up Exercise (Optional)

To introduce players to rules and dynamics of the exercise, have four players stand, facing the center, as shown below.

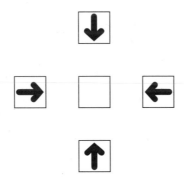

Have the rest of the team observe while the four players move to the other side following the Player Instructions.

Step 6: Game Play

This step outlines the actual conduct of the game.

Preliminaries

- Select a team of eight players, divided into two subgroups of four each. If you have additional players, assign the following roles:

  Observer, to record reactions of players.

  Judge, to ensure that players abide by the rules.

- Instruct each subgroup to stand on one row of newspaper squares, leaving the middle space unoccupied.

- Make sure all players face toward the center square, as shown below.

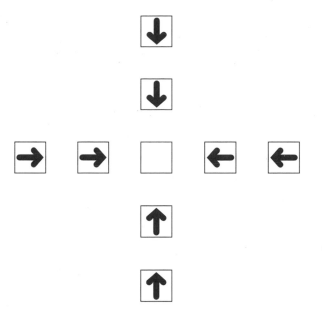

Start Game Play

- Post the Player Instructions and inform players they must cross to the other side of road.

- Players may talk with one another during game play.

- If players want to hold a planning meeting, allow for a time out. Players may leave the game area for any meeting. (Teams may want to use a flip chart to plan their moves.) After the meeting, have team reassemble on their starting spaces.

- Continue play until teams have crossed to the other side or you feel it is time to stop the game for discussion or team meetings.

Step 7: Closure/Debriefing

End the game and debrief the learning experience.

Closure

If teams successfully crossed the road, congratulate all players. Use this time to discuss problems with the game in terms of rules, questions, or team play. If there were disagreements among players during the game, ask if the disagreements were handled productively or not. If not, what would have worked? Now is the time to look at the game to gain a prospective of what happened and what can be taken back to the workplace.

Debriefing

Debriefing is the process of helping people reflect on their experiences to find meaningful learning. It usually takes place immediately after the game experience. Guided debriefing involves the facilitator initiating and moderating the discussion. The debriefing period can include discussion of the game solution(s) or venting, with learners letting off steam. The debriefing period should also promote shared insights and generalizations about the relationship of the game and its content to real life and the workplace.

Most instructors have their own method of debriefing, but may wish to follow a debriefing process of "What?" "So what?" and "Now what?" as demonstrated with the following questions.

What? What did you experience?

- How did you feel when you first saw the Cross Roads game area?

- How did you feel when you had problems crossing the road?

- What happened when your team was blocked?

- Do you think a team meeting would have helped?

- If you held a team meeting, did it help? In what way?

- Did talk during play help or hinder your problem solving? In what way?

- What happened, chronologically?

So What? What learning happened?

- What critical incidents in the game led to some insight about your team's functioning?

- What did you learn from the readings or lecture?

- What one major idea or concept did you gain from the experience?

- What on-the-job experiences did playing this game remind you of or seem to be related to?

Now What? What associations can be made between the game and real life and the work-place?

- How does this game relate to real life?

- How does the "floor" experience relate to real life? To the workplace?

- From your experiences here, what different behaviors would you show at the next meeting or group problem-solving session your team holds?

- What if different people from your organization were present?

● PART TWO ●

....

21 Team Games

....

Book at a Glance

Skill to Teach / Team Model	Team Spirit	Cutting Edge	Traditional	Task Force	Cyber Teams
Coaching	Bell Hop	Bell Hop Line Up	Bell Hop Line Up	Bell Hop Line Up	
Cooperation/ Competition	Box of Chocolates Buzz Word Tooth and Nail	Box of Chocolates Buzz Word Super Model Tooth and Nail	Box of Chocolates Buzz Word Super Model Tooth and Nail	Box of Chocolates Buzz Word Super Model Tooth and Nail	Buzz Word ww.where and ww.when
Creativity	Buzz Word Cross Roads	Buzz Word Cross Roads	Buzz Word Cross Roads	Buzz Word Cross Roads	Buzz Word ww.where and ww.when
Decision Making	Duel Identity	Duel Identity	Duel Identity	Duel Identity	ww.where and ww.when
Feedback	Bell Hop Box of Chocolates Regards Sentence Prompt Snow Ball	Bell Hop Box of Chocolates Regards Sentence Prompt Snow Ball	Bell Hop Box of Chocolates Regards Sentence Prompt Snow Ball	Bell Hop Box of Chocolates Regards Sentence Prompt Snow Ball	Bell Hop Sentence Prompt

Skill to Teach / Team Model	Team Spirit	Cutting Edge	Traditional	Task Force	Cyber Teams
Goal Setting	Box of Chocolates Match Point	Box of Chocolates Match Point RAT Race	Box of Chocolates Match Point RAT Race	Box of Chocolates Match Point RAT Race	Match Point ww.where and ww.when
Icebreakers	Buzz Word High Five Name That Team Pass the Buck Regards Snow Ball Team Roast	Buzz Word High Five Name That Team Pass the Buck Regards Snow Ball Team Roast	Buzz Word High Five Name That Team Pass the Buck Regards Snow Ball Team Roast	Buzz Word High Five Name That Team Pass the Buck Regards Snow Ball Team Roast	Buzz Word High Five Name That Team Team Roast
Leadership/ Authority		Cross Roads Line Up Power Tag	Cross Roads Line Up Power Tag	Cross Roads Line Up Power Tag	ww.where and ww.when
Managing Conflict		Cross Roads Power Tag	Cross Roads Power Tag	Cross Roads Power Tag	
Meeting Management		RAT Race	RAT Race	RAT Race	ww.where and ww.when
Norms	Norman Says!	Norman Says! RAT Race	Norman Says! RAT Race	Norman Says! RAT Race	
Planning	Bell Hop Pass the Buck	Bell Hop Pass the Buck Super Model	Bell Hop Pass the Buck Super Model	Bell Hop Pass the Buck Super Model	Bell Hop ww.where and ww.when
Problem Solving	Brain Frame Buzz Word	Brain Frame Buzz Word	Brain Frame Buzz Word	Brain Frame Buzz Word	Brain Frame Buzz Word

Skill to Teach / Team Model	Team Spirit	Cutting Edge	Traditional	Task Force	Cyber Teams
Problem Solving (cont.)	Duel Identity Sentence Prompt	Duel Identity Line Up RAT Race Sentence Prompt Super Model	Duel Identity Line Up RAT Race Sentence Prompt Super Model	Duel Identity Line Up RAT Race Sentence Prompt Super Model	Sentence Prompt ww.where and ww.when
Role Clarification		RAT Race	RAT Race	RAT Race	
Team Communication	Bell Hop Box of Chocolates Regards	Bell Hop Box of Chocolates Cross Roads Norman Says! Regards Super Model	Bell Hop Box of Chocolates Cross Roads Norman Says! Regards Super Model	Bell Hop Box of Chocolates Cross Roads Norman Says! Regards Super Model	Bell Hop
Team Learning	Cross Roads RAT Race	Cross Roads RAT Race	Cross Roads RAT Race	Cross Roads RAT Race	Cross Roads ww.where and ww.when
Trust	Duel Identity Power Tag Tooth and Nail	Duel Identity Power Tag Tooth and Nail	Duel Identity Power Tag Tooth and Nail	Duel Identity Power Tag Tooth and Nail	
Types of Teams	High Five Name That Team Team Roast	High Five Name That Team Team Roast	High Five Name That Team Team Roast	High Five Name That Team Team Roast	High Five Name That Team Team Roast

● NOTE ABOUT CYBER TEAMS

Getting On-Line to Play

- One game in this book, ww.where and ww.when, is specifically written to be played on-line. Some of the other games can also be played on-line if you have access to e-mail, chat, and conferencing functions. These games are:

  Bell Hop

  Brain Frame

  Buzz Word

  Cross Roads

  Team Roast

  Other games not on this list would be appropriate if the cyber team were meeting face-to-face.

- Many search engine services are now giving away free e-mail services. E-mail is a function that is almost automatic if you are signed up with an Internet Service Provider (ISP).

You can obtain a free chat function by pointing your browser to *http://www.icq.com* and following the instructions that are posted there.

You can obtain free conferencing functionality by pointing your browser to *http://web.eesite.com* and following the instructions that are posted there.

If you do the above, your team will then have e-mail, chat, and conferencing functions that can be used to play the games listed above over the Internet.

Bell Hop

• •

● PURPOSE

- To demonstrate the planning and cooperation required for teamwork.

- To demonstrate the dynamics of feedback in teamwork and its role in productivity.

- To practice effective communication in a team environment.

● TIME

Twenty-five minutes.

● PLAYERS

Eight or more.

● SUPPLIES

- An overhead transparency or newsprint flip-chart page of the Player Instructions for Bell Hop, prepared in advance by the facilitator.

- An overhead projector (if using a transparency).

- Twenty-one newspaper sections or large pieces of cardboard. (The back portion of a newsprint pad can provide four to six pieces of cardboard.)

- Two blindfolds made from pieces of folded cloth or purchased from a medical supply house.

- Two dinner bells, chimes, or noisemakers.

- A newsprint flip chart and felt-tipped markers.

- Masking tape, to hold down newspapers or cardboard, as necessary.

● STEPS

1. Divide the group into two teams.

2. Set up a path of sixteen newspaper sections or pieces of cardboard in a straight line, as shown below.

3. Define the task: "Each team selects a representative. The two representatives will be blindfolded and placed at opposite ends of the path. Each team must guide its representative to the other end of the path using only a bell, chime, or another type of noisemaker. You may not speak to one another. Rules of passage:

   a. Representatives may only move forward.

   b. Two representatives may not stand on the same space.

   c. Representatives may not step off the path. If either steps off the path, he or she must be returned to the starting point.

   The game is over when both representatives have successfully moved to the opposite ends of the path. Players have fifteen minutes to move from one end to the other."

4. Ask each team to hold a meeting and select a representative.

5. Post the Player Instructions, and begin the game.

6. Ask each representative to stand at one end of the path. Instruct a team member to blindfold each representative.

7. When each team has blindfolded its representative, remind teams that no talking is allowed for the rest of the game.

8. Place the last five newspapers on the floor, as shown below:

9. Inform players they have fifteen minutes to cross to the other side.

10. Play continues until the two players have passed to the other side or until time is called.

● FACILITATOR NOTES FOR BELL HOP

- Do not force anyone to be blindfolded. Many people become stressed out when blindfolded. Only use volunteers. If there are no volunteers, do not play the game.

- This game is especially useful for teams whose members work at a distance from one another. For them it will highlight the phenomenon of not having been told the full instructions or goals for a project. This is especially true if part of the team works in an office and the rest of the team works at a distance. The people who work in the office may know something about what mechanisms there are to keep the team members who are at a distance informed on a regular basis.

- Debrief the blindfolded people first. They have been under the most stress and may feel that they have been tricked. If this is true, then they need time to process what has happened to them.

- It is important to ask the people who were blindfolded what feedback was useful and what feedback was not useful. Sometimes the person giving the feedback thinks that he or she is giving feedback in a constructive manner; however, it may not be considered useful by the person receiving it. Two good questions to ask the people who were blindfolded are, "What kind of feedback would have been useful to you" and "How would you like to have received that feedback?"

- A few questions that would be pertinent to this game follow:

  a. In what way do you feel blindfolded at work?

b. What are the consequences of being blindfolded at work?

c. What can be done to keep the blindfold off at work?

d. What does what you have done here mean for the operations of your team?

● CUSTOMIZING BELL HOP

Regarding Group Size

- For larger groups, prepare two or more paths, then divide the group into two or more sets of teams. Assign a player-facilitator to guide each game.

Regarding Time

- Shorten or lengthen times for the meeting and rounds of play.

Regarding Focus of the Task

- Have one team use a dinner bell; have the other team use another type of noisemaker, such as a clicker or a whistle.

- Allow teams to hold additional planning meetings, as necessary.

- Inform teams of "standard" crossing time.

- Stop the game when the first team representative crosses to the other side. Conduct a quick debriefing and then start another game. Compare the outcomes.

- Have two blindfolded representatives stand, one behind the other, and do the crossing like a train. This should require more coordination.

- Stop the game to allow the teams to give two additional instructions to their blindfolded representatives. Then continue play.

Bell Hop

....

- **Divide into two teams.**

- **Blindfold one player on your team.**

- **Place your blindfolded player on one end of the path.**

- **Guide your blindfolded player to the other end of the path using ONLY the bell.**

Box of Chocolates

● ●

● **PURPOSE**

- To demonstrate the difference between cooperation and competition.

- To demonstrate the effectiveness of goal specification.

- To evaluate team communications.

● **TIME**

Twenty minutes.

● **PLAYERS**

Six or more.

● **SUPPLIES**

- An overhead transparency or newsprint flip-chart page of the Player Instructions for Box of Chocolates, prepared in advance by the facilitator.

- An overhead projector (if using a transparency).

- One set of game sheets for each team, prepared in advance by the facilitator.

- A newsprint flip chart and felt-tipped markers.

- Paper and pencils for each team.

● STEPS

1. Divide the group into sets of two teams. Have each set of teams face each other at a conference table or seating area.

2. Distribute game sheets, paper, and pencils to each team.

3. Define the task: "This game requires you to find three truffles on your opponent's game sheet by identifying what is in one space (number and letter) at a time. The opposing team will indicate whether the space contains a 'regular' chocolate or a 'truffle.' Play alternates after each guess. Play continues until one team finds the other team's three truffles."

4. Have each team select three spaces on the Your Team's Box of Chocolates portion of the game sheet and mark those spaces with a "T" to designate the three "truffles."

5. Post the Player Instructions, and begin the game.

6. The first team to locate the other team's three truffles wins.

● FACILITATOR NOTES

• This game will highlight the impact of various ways of giving feedback. It provides a great springboard for the team members to discuss how they give feedback at work and how they could improve the process.

• The game will also provide an opportunity to discuss how much information team members should share with one another. There are those who think that only the major points should be shared. Others think that everything they know should be shared. This would be an opportunity for a team to discuss how they want feedback to work on their team.

• This game can be used to observe the impact of guarded and open communication. If one team just says "truffle" or "chocolate," but the other team gives additional information, such as "You're getting hot," what happens to the exchange? If Team A gives more information, saying, "You are three spaces away," will Team B start to share more information? If Team B does not reciprocate, will Team A start giving less information? Does either side change? If so, why? Do they stay the same? If so, why?

a. If this is viewed as a win-lose situation, then both teams will try to keep information sharing to an absolute minimum.

b. If this is viewed as a win-win situation, then teams should be providing more feedback than just saying "chocolate" or "truffle."

- Sometimes the urge to win is so strong that a team may begin to shade the truth a little. Team A may intentionally mislead Team B so that Team A can win. When Team B finds out that it has been misled, the trust between the two teams diminishes. The diminishment of trust is not productive for either inter- or intra-team cooperation.

  If any shading of the truth occurs, it will give you an opportunity to discuss the issue of trust and its impact on team relationships. Also, a discussion on how trust can be restored once it has been destroyed would be useful.

● CUSTOMIZING BOX OF CHOCOLATES

Regarding Group Size

- For smaller groups, divide participants into one set of two teams.

Regarding Time

- Shorten or lengthen times for meeting and round of play.

Regarding Focus of the Task

- Continue play until both teams find the three "truffles."

- Have both teams place only one truffle on the game sheet. Determine whether the "lucky guess" factor adds or detracts from the game play.

- Limit the number of guesses to seven. Determine how many truffles have been located. Conduct a discussion, as appropriate, then continue play until one team locates the three truffles.

- Conduct a "play off" tournament in which winning teams play one another until only one team is undefeated. Discuss how additional competition affected quality of play.

Box of Chocolates

- Divide into sets of two teams.

- As a team decide where to place three "truffles" on the Your Team portion of the game sheet.

- Take turns with your opposing team guessing the location of the three "truffles" on your game sheets.

- Play until one team has located the three "truffles" on the other's game sheet.

GAME SHEET FOR
Box of Chocolates

....

Your Team's Box of Chocolates

1. The grids below represent boxes of chocolates. Select three spaces on your team's grid to represent truffles. Place a "T" in each space without letting the other team see your board.

2. Record the other team's guesses for each of their turns below and also mark them on your game sheet.

Turn	Space
1	

	A	B	C	D	E	F
1						
2						
3						
4						
5						
6						

Other Team's Box of Chocolates

1. Record your own guesses about the other team's truffles on the chart below.

2. Mark the game sheet with a "C" for every regular chocolate and "T" for truffle you locate on the other team's grid.

Turn	Space
1	

	A	B	C	D	E	F
1						
2						
3						
4						
5						
6						

Brain Frame

• •

● PURPOSE

- To motivate participants to create as many options as possible for learning topics.

- To demonstrate an easy brainstorming structure.

- To demonstrate a brainstorming method that helps unblock thinking.

- To demonstrate a method to get people to think outside of the box.

● TIME

Thirty minutes.

● PLAYERS

Nine or more.

● SUPPLIES

- An overhead transparency or newsprint flip-chart page of the Player Instructions for Brain Frame, prepared in advance by the facilitator.

- An overhead projector (if using a transparency).

- One flip-chart size Game Sheet for Brain Frame for each team, prepared in advance by the facilitator.

- One set of fine-tipped markers for each team.

- Masking tape, to post game sheets, as necessary.

● STEPS

1. Divide the group into teams of three to five players each. Have each team meet at one of the posted game sheets.

2. Define the task: "This is a structured form of brainstorming in which teams will use a matrix that shows a letter across the horizontal axis and a category along the vertical axis. The game requires teams to come up with as many items as possible containing one or two words, as suggested by the letter and category on the matrix. Each correctly identified item will receive 1 point. In addition, any correct item *not* found on any opponent's list will receive a bonus of 3 points. A round consists of seven minutes. The team with the most points at the end of the round wins."

3. Post the Player Instructions, and begin the game.

4. At the end of seven minutes go over the teams' game sheets and award appropriate points.

● SCORING EXAMPLE

Brainstorming Topic: Improving Plant Safety

1. Teams A and B have game sheets with the letters A, M, and P along the horizontal axis and the categories clothing, materials, and activities along the vertical axis.

2. Teams start play. At the end of seven minutes time is called.

3. Team A tallies its items:

   a. *15 clothing:* ace bandage, arm bands, asbestos gloves, aprons, argyle socks, ascot, mad-cap, masks, moccasins, moleskin pants, mouth piece, Panama hat, pantaloons, pressure suit, painter's pants

   b. *17 materials:* asbestos, acoustical, aerosol spray, air brush, alligator clips, aluminum, ammonia, antiseptic spray, mace, machine guards, median strips, microscope, paddle, particle board, pepper spray, peroxide, pesticides

c. *9 activities:* Award Days, accident prevention, adequate training, aerobics, artificial respiration, auditory testing, mentor program, performance test, phone tree

Team A's preliminary score = 15 + 17 + 9 = 41 points.

4. Team B tallies its items:

a. *12 clothing:* ace bandage, argyle socks, alligator shoes, apron, mouth piece, mouth guard, muffler, muslin shirt, pea jacket, pearls, pith helmet, purse

b. *14 materials:* abrasive, acid testers, activated charcoal, aerosol spray, ash trays, methane, particle board, pepper spray, peroxide, pesticides, phone, pipe wrench, pinstripe, pocket knife

c. *12 activities:* AIDS prevention, aisle clearance, anonymous suggestions, accident prevention, adequate training, aerobics, arm wrestle, artificial respiration, auditory testing, mentor program, performance test, phone tree

Team B's preliminary score = 12 + 14 + 12 = 38 points.

5. Facilitator reviews both game sheets and awards bonus points.

a. Team A items *not* found on opponent's list:

11 clothing

12 materials

1 activity

Team A receives (11 + 12 + 1) x 3 points = 72 points

Team A's final score = 41 + 72 bonus points = 113 points

b. Team B items *not* found on opponent's list:

8 clothing

9 materials

4 activities

Team B receives (8 + 9 + 4) x 3 points = 63 points

Team B's final score = 38 + 63 bonus points = 101 points.

6. Team A is declared the winner of the round.

- For some groups, a free-form approach to brainstorming does not work very well. In the traditional free-form type of brainstorming, individuals in the group may spend time evaluating the suggestions in their own minds and not sharing everything they are thinking. The group may also engage in judgmental behavior and prevent good ideas from being written down. Brain Frame will force individuals and the group to think of ideas in a way that minimizes judgmental behavior.

- Most people do some warm-up exercises before they jump into heavy exercising. Runners do stretching exercises for their leg muscles. By doing the warm-ups, people have an easier time doing the exercise.

  There should be stretching exercises for our brain also. Before you have groups begin brainstorming about a particular topic, give them a few fun warm-up brainstorms. For example, brainstorm how many uses there are for a flip chart, a piece of newspaper, a safety pin, a marker, a pair of shoes, etc.

- The letters and words given in this game are just suggestions. Create your own frame with the letters and words you think will best help the team. Do not worry if you cannot think of a word or idea to put into each box of the frame you create. Just because you cannot think of a word does not mean that the team playing the game will not be able to think of one or more.

- If the group objects to the words and letters you have used, create a new chart with their words and letters. Keep your chart, however. The words and the ideas they generate may not help solve the problem. After they try their own words and letters, they may be willing to use yours.

- If there is a chat room function or a conference room function available on your computer network, this game can also be played by a cyber team. Someone would have to serve as a recorder to write down the words and ideas, create the matrix using a spreadsheet program, and then post it for everyone else to see.

- One of the hindrances to a good brainstorming session is the censoring that people do internally or externally. When internal censoring is operating, people will not mention something that they see as senseless or useless or maybe just a little strange. External censoring is in operation when people refuse to write ideas that they do not agree with or that they think will not work. Both forms of censoring hinder the potential payoff from a brainstorming session.

- To help people to ignore the censoring, give prizes to the team that lists the most items. Remember that brainstorming is used for *quantity* of ideas, not quality. Quality will come later.

- Try using two initial brainstorming sessions about topics not related to the problem and give prizes—such as pencils, coffee mugs, balloons, or bottles of bubbles. This generally results in an increase in ideas in the main round.

- In the authors' experience, the first round usually produces between thirty and forty ideas, the second between fifty and seventy. For the third round, groups usually come up with over one hundred ideas on how to solve the real problem.

● CUSTOMIZING BRAIN FRAME

Regarding Group Size

- Divide smaller groups into two teams.

- Use additional game sheets for larger groups. Allow for more time to discuss and process listed items.

Regarding Time

- Shorten or lengthen the time for a round of play.

- Expand or contract the number of categories and letters.

Regarding Focus of the Task

- Use words on both axes to make the challenge more difficult.

- Use numbers or dates on the horizontal axis instead of letters. Teams can use the Brain Frame grid to identify stages, dates, or milestones of a project or process.

- Create random rounds by placing letters in one hat and categories in another, then have teams draw to create a random brainstorming round.

- Use game sheets as a take-home to reinforce reading assignments by having everyone fill them out after reading the material.

- Make everyone a "recorder" by distributing felt-tipped markers to all players. This also removes the imposed leadership role assumed by having only one recorder for a team.

- Accommodate different categories or numbers of topics by using different matrix designs, such as 2 x 2, 2 x 3, or 3 x 4.

- Rotate game sheets among the teams for each round of play. Continue this until all teams have played on all game sheets.

Regarding Scoring

- Award ten bonus points to each team that places at least one item in each square on the game sheet.

Brain Frame

- Divide into teams.

- Develop a list of as many items as possible suggested by the categories and letters for each grid on the game sheet.

- Receive 1 point for each item and a bonus of 3 points for each item that no other team uses.

Brain Frame

Improving Plant Safety

	A	M	P
Clothing			
Materials			
Activities			

Buzz Word

● ●

● **PURPOSE**

- To demonstrate intra-team cooperation and planning.

- To practice team problem solving.

- To explore behavior needed for creativity in a team setting.

● **TIME**

Twenty-five minutes.

● **PLAYERS**

Twelve or more.

● **SUPPLIES**

- An overhead transparency or newsprint flip-chart page of the Player Instructions for Buzz Word, prepared in advance by the facilitator.

- An overhead projector (if using a transparency).

- One sheet of newsprint and felt-tipped markers for each team.

- Masking tape to hang the lists.

- One set of five letter cards (different cards for each team), prepared in advance by the facilitator. The cards should be made on index stock, with one letter on both sides of each card. The facilitator should prepare one set of cards per round for each team for up to three rounds of play. For example, prepare fifteen different sets of cards for five teams playing three rounds.

- One Sample List of Buzz Words with possible three-letter, four-letter, and five-letter word combinations using the letters assigned.

- One standard dictionary for reference during the game.

- A calculator for each recorder (optional).

● STEPS

1. Divide the group into teams of six players each.

2. Distribute one sheet of newsprint paper and felt-tipped markers to each team.

3. Have each team select one player to serve as a recorder to document the words formed during play and tally the final score at the end of each round.

4. Have teams swap recorders after each round to encourage equity of play.

5. Define the task: "Each team will be given one set of five cards, each with one letter written on both sides. Each card is assigned to one player. The team has two minutes to form words of three or more letters using only the letters on the cards. Each word is formed by the players holding their letters in proper order so that the word can be read by the recorder. Once the recorder writes the word on the newsprint, the team can form the next word. When play stops, the recorder tallies the total points earned from the words formed."

6. Scoring. Points are earned only for words of three, four, or five letters:

   a. Five-letter words earn 17 points.

   b. Four-letter words earn 10 points.

   c. Three-letter words earn 5 points.

7. Post the Player Instructions, and begin the game.

8. Stop play at the end of two minutes. Have recorders display their lists for all to see.

9. Go over each list of words and double check the recorders' tallies.

10. Play one or two additional rounds, time and enthusiasm permitting.

11. At the end of the final round, total each team's points. Declare the team with the most points the winner.

● SCORING EXAMPLE

1. Team A receives the letters A, B, D, E, and R. Team B receives the letters A, C, H, R, and S.

2. The facilitator starts the first round of play.

3. Team A forms its first word, "bad." The recorder writes the word on the newsprint. Team A forms another word, "bed," and the recorder writes down the second word. This process continues until time is called. Team A's recorder has the following list: "bad, bed, bard, beard, bread, red, bare, bear, and dab."

4. At the same time, Team B has been forming words from its letters: a, c, h, r, and s. Team B's recorder has written the following list: "car, ash, arc, has, arch, cars, cash, rash, and crash."

5. Play is stopped. Recorders tally points and post their newsprint sheets.

6. The facilitator reviews Team A's sheet and awards points as follows:

2 @ 5 letters (beard, bread) = 2 @ 17 =	34 points
3 @ 4 letters (bear, bard, bare) = 3 @ 10 =	30 points
4 @ 3 letters (bad, bed, red, dab) = 4 @ 5 =	20 points
Team A total score =	84 points

7. Facilitator reviews Team B's list of words and awards points as follows:

1 @ 5 letters (crash) = 1 @ 17 =	17 points
4 @ 4 letters (arch, cars, cash, rash) = 4 @ 10 =	40 points
5 @ 3 letters (arc, ash, car, has, sac) = 5 @ 5 =	25 points
Team B total score =	82 points

8. Team A is declared the winner of Round 1.

● FACILITATOR NOTES

- Although not stated, teams will find they can form the words more quickly when standing and moving about. This is a good reason to play this game right after lunch. It will get people moving, keep them out of their seats, and energize them. Use this game whenever the team seems to have low energy or seems to be stuck on a problem.

- People who move around a lot during the day on their jobs get tired and drained from sitting all day. An exercise like this keeps them moving to solve the problem.

- The key to this game is to have people look at what behaviors helped them solve the problem and whether any of those behaviors can be applicable back on the job. Ask: "What behaviors helped solve the problem?" "What behaviors increased communication?"

- This would also be an appropriate game to use as a warmup for brainstorming.

- This game can also be played with a Cyber team if everyone is in a chat room. Each member could post the words they formed. Team members could also tell a central person how to rearrange the letters. The action is really exciting if there are two teams in the same chat room and people have to pay attention to which posting is for them and which is for the other team.

● CUSTOMIZING BUZZ WORD

Regarding Group Size

- Have smaller groups act as one team.

- Use four-letter sets for smaller groups or to introduce play. Suggested scoring: 10 points for four-letter words, 5 points for three-letter words, and 2 points for two-letter words.

Regarding Time

- Shorten or lengthen time for a round of play.

Regarding Focus of the Task

- Select words of special importance to the topic that can be formed from the assigned letters. Inform players that if a team forms a secret buzz word during play, they will receive a 25-point bonus. Reveal the secret word only during scoring.

- Write all five letters on one 3" x 5" index card. Give one index card to each team. Have team members individually call out words that can be formed as the recorder writes them down. At the end of the round have recorders tally the score.

- Create cards that depict parts of a process. Then ask the team to put the parts together in a way that makes sense, but not necessarily in the same order they are used to. This often presents the process in a different, and often revealing, perspective.

- Increase the difficulty of letter combinations in each successive round.

Regarding Scoring

- Change the scoring. Increase points earned for five-letter words to 25. Change points earned for all words to 5 points.

Buzz Word

....

- Divide into teams of six.

- You have two minutes to form words of three or more letters using the letters assigned to you.

- Words earn the following scores:

    Five-letter words = 17 points *10*

    Four-letter words = 10 points *5*

    Three-letter words = 5 points *2*

SAMPLE LIST FOR
Buzz Word

....

a, e, l, p, s (33)

five-letter words: lapse, leaps, pales, peals, pleas, sepal

four-letter words: ales, alps, apes, apse, laps, leap, leas, pale, pals, peal, peas, plea, sale, seal, slap

three-letter words: ale, alp, ape, asp, lap, lea, pal, pas, pea, sap, sea, spa

a, b, e, s, t (29)

five-letter words: abets, baste, bates, beast, beats

four-letter words: abet, base, bast, bate, bats, beat, best, bets, east, eats, sate, seat, stab, tabs, teas

three-letter words: ate, bat, bet, eat, sat, sea, set, tab, tea

a, b, d, e, r (27)

five-letter words: bared, beard, bread, debar

four-letter words: abed, bad, bard, bare, bead, bear, brad, brae, bred, dare, dear, drab, read

three-letter words: are, bad, bar, bed, bra, dab, deb, ear, era, red

a, e, m, r, s (24)

five-letter words: mares, maser, reams, smear

four-letter words: arms, ears, eras, mare, mars, mesa, rams, ream, same, seam, sear, sera

three-letter words: are, ares, arm, ear, era, mare, ram, sea

1. a, e, g, r, t (23) *Green*

    five-letter words: grate, great

    four-letter words: gate, gear, rage, rate, tare, tear

    three-letter words: age, are, art, ate, ear, eat, era, gar, get, rag, rat, reg, tag, tar, tea

2. a, e, f, s, t (23) *Red*

    five-letter words: fates, feast, feats

    four-letter words: east, eats, efts, fast, fate, fats, feat, safe, sate, seat, teas

    three-letter words: aft, ate, eat, eft, fat, sat, sea, set, tea

e, i, r, s, t (21)

    five-letter words: rites, tiers, tires, tries

    four-letter words: erst, ires, rest, rise, rite, sire, site, stir, tier, ties, tire

    three-letter words: ire, its, set, sir, sit, tie

a, e, i, l, s (17)

    five-letter word: aisle

    four-letter words: ails, ales, ilea, isle, leas, leis, lies, sail, sale, seal

    three-letter words: ail, ale, lea, lei, lie, sea

a, e, r, t, t (17)

    five-letter words: tetra, treat

    four-letter words: rate, tare, tart, tear, teat

    three-letter words: are, art, ate, ear, eat, era, rat, tar, tat, tea

Jossey-Bass/Pfeiffer

e, h, o, r, s (17)

  five-letter words: heros, horse, shore

  four-letter words: hers, hero, hoes, hose, ores, roes, rose, shoe, sore

  three-letter words: her, hoe, ore, roe, she

a, e, f, m, r (16)

  five-letter word: frame

  four-letter words: fame, fare, farm, fear, mare, ream,

  three-letter words: are, arm, ear, emf, era, far, mar, ram, ref

a, e, g, m, s (15)

  five-letter word: games

  four-letter words: ages, game, gems, mags, mesa, sage, same, seam

  three-letter words: age, gas, gem, mag, sag, sea

a, e, l, n, r (14)

  five-letter words: learn, renal

  four-letter words: earl, earn, lane, lean, near, real

  three-letter words: ale, arc, ear, era, lea, ran

a, c, h, r, s (14)

  five-letter words: chars, crash

  four-letter words: arch, arcs, cars, cash, char, rash, scar

  three-letter words: arc, ash, car, has, sac

e, i, h, t, w (13)

    five-letter words: white, withe

    four-letter words: thew, whet, whit, with,

    three-letter words: hew, hie, hit, the, tie, wet, wit,

f, i, r, s, t (13)

    five-letter words: first, rifts

    four-letter words: firs, fist, fits, rift, sift, stir

    three-letter words: fir, fit, its, sir, sit

e, g, o, r, u (13)

    five-letter words: rogue, rouge

    four-letter words: ergo, gore, ogre, urge

    three-letter words: ego, ore, our, reg, roe, rue, rug

a, f, l, o, t (13)

    five-letter words: aloft, float,

    four-letter words: alto, flat, foal, loaf, loft

    three-letter words: aft, fat, lot, oaf, oat, oft

a, c, d, e, n (13)

    five-letter words: caned, dance

    four-letter words: aced, acne, cane, dace, dean

    three-letter words: ace, and, cad, can, den, end

h, o, r, t, w (12)

five-letter words:	throw, worth, wroth
four-letter word:	wort
three-letter words:	hot, how, rot, row, tor, tow, two, who

a, g, r, s, u (9)

five-letter word:	sugar
four-letter words:	gars, rags, rugs
three-letter words:	gar, gas, rag, rug, sag

f, h, o, r, t (9)

five-letter words:	forth, froth
four-letter word:	fort
three-letter words:	for, fro, hot, oft, rot, tor

d, o, r, s, w (9)

five-letter words:	sword, words
four-letter words:	rods, rows, word
three-letter words:	rod, row, sod, sow

a, b, c, l, k (8)

five-letter word:	black
four-letter words:	back, balk, calk, lack
three-letter words:	cab, lab, lac

a, d, l, n, s (7)

      five-letter word: lands

      four-letter words: lads, land, sand

      three-letter words: and, lad, sad

a, c, g, i, m (6)

      five-letter word: magic

      four-letter words: magi, mica

      three-letter words: aim, cam, mag

Cross Roads

· ·

● PURPOSE

- To demonstrate the importance of team communication.

- To demonstrate how a team manages shared memory.

- To demonstrate how a team solves problems and thinks "outside the box."

- To demonstrate inter-team conflict and how conflict reduces team resources.

● TIME

Thirty minutes.

● PLAYERS

Eight or more.

● SUPPLIES

- An overhead transparency or newsprint flip-chart page of the Player Instructions for Cross Roads, prepared in advance by the facilitator.

- An overhead projector (if using a transparency).

- Nine large squares made from newspaper sections or large pieces of cardboard. The back portion of a newsprint pad can provide four to six squares.

- A newsprint flip chart and felt-tipped markers.

- Masking tape, to hold down newspapers or cardboard, as necessary.

● STEPS

1. Set up a floor plan of nine newspaper sections or pieces of cardboard in squares, as shown below.

2. Have the group select two sets of four players. The rest of the players may act as observers and judges.

3. Define the task: "This game requires two sets of four players to cross to the other side of the road. One player stands on each section, leaving the center space open. All players line up facing toward the center space.

Legal Moves

- A player may move into an empty space in front of him or her.

- A player may move around a person who is facing him or her into an empty space.

- Only one player may move at a time.

Illegal Moves

- A player may not move backward.

- A player may not move around someone facing the same way as he or she is, that is, if the player would be looking at the other person's back prior to the move.

- Two players may not move at the same time.

- Two players cannot occupy the same space at the same time.

- No player may step off of the game.

4. Instruct the teams to meet for five minutes to plan.

5. Post the Player Instructions, and begin the game.

6. Play continues until all players have crossed to the other side or until time is called.

● FACILITATOR NOTES

- This exercise is usually frustrating to the participants until they hit on the solution. The facilitator must keep focused on the process. If the process is good, a solution will be found.

- When the participants become frustrated, here are some questions that will come in handy to help them out.

  What are you doing?

  Is it working?

  What might you try differently?

  Do you have to stay standing on the space? [Only ask this question if the teams have tried to solve the problem about four times and are not making progress.]

- The point here is to show the team how it can become stuck in a certain mode of operation and that by changing that mode of operation it can get "out of the box" for a fresh perspective.

  a. Some teams will gather around a flip chart or white board and draw the problem and try to solve it there first.

  b. Some teams will get pencils or pens and line them up and try to move them through the steps to try to solve the problem.

c. By using one of the two methods above, the participants get the total picture of the problem and not just the perspective they had while standing on the newspaper. This gives them a "big picture" view. You can then ask the participants whether they find it helpful to step away and how they could apply that process at work.

- If a team is having difficulty, you may notice that some people start to drift away from the newspaper on the floor. Some will try to get more involved in the process, others will sit down and watch what is happening, and some may even pick up a book to read. What is happening can be looked at from two different learning perspectives, as given below.

Learning Point One

The conflict occurring within the team and its inability to solve the problem causes members of the team either to become more involved or to drift away. An excellent discussion can be conducted by asking people on each team why they did what they did.

- Why did you get closer to the action?

- Why did you move away from the action?

- What happens when both behaviors occur within a team?

- What does this mean for keeping the whole team involved in solving problems?

An important teaching point is that the team must be conscious of when it starts to lose team members/resources and take action to reverse that trend. To allow members to drift away will weaken a team.

Learning Point Two

You will hear a lot of discussion about how to solve the problem, and you will notice that no one is writing anything down. As a result you will hear the same thing being said more than once. Suggestions are made, but because they are not recorded, they are promptly forgotten. The learning point here is how to keep a team's joint memory.

Some answers to that question include writing things down, conducting a formal brainstorming session, and reacting to each suggestion as it is mentioned rather than letting it "plop." (A "plop" is when someone says something and no one responds. A team with a lot of "plops" begins to smell of failure.)

You can easily expand on this point to discuss how a team communicates: How much is written down? How much is spoken? and How does the team preserve its common memory? Material on team learning from Chapter 12 in Peter Senge's *The Fifth Discipline* would be helpful here.

Here are some additional questions you can use to process this game:

- What happened?

- How do you feel about the activity?

- What did the activity mean for you?

- What did you learn about teamwork?

- What decisions were made and by whom?

- What helped give you the solution?

- Where were you stuck, and how did you get unstuck?

- What kind of group support was there for your decisions?

- Who had ideas not expressed, not listened to?

- What significance does what happened in your team have at work, at home, in your association?

Reference

Senge, P.M. (1990). *The fifth discipline*. New York: Doubleday/Currency.

1. Players line up in the start sequence:

1

2

5   6   ☐   7   8

3

4

2. The horizontal line (5, 6, 7, 8) crosses to the opposite side in eight moves:

Move 1	5 . 6 7 8
Move 2	5 7 6 . 8
Move 3	5 7 6 8 .
Move 4	5 7 . 8 6
Move 5	. 7 5 8 6
Move 6	7 . 5 8 6
Move 7	7 8 5 . 6
Move 8	7 8 . 5 6

3. The vertical line (1, 2, 3, 4) crosses to the opposite side using the same sequence of moves.

4. The key to solving the puzzle is that teams alternate movements.

● CUSTOMIZING CROSS ROADS

Regarding Group Size

- Assign extra players roles as judges and observers.

Regarding Time

- Shorten or lengthen times for planning meetings and for rounds of play.

Regarding Focus of the Task

- Set up the game for twelve players. Allow additional time for planning and game play.

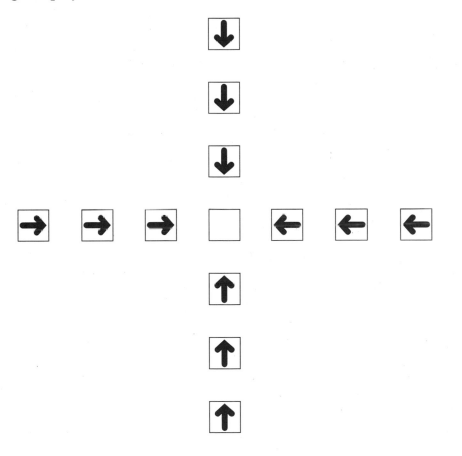

- Allow one or two extra players to act as "floor supervisors" to counsel players, diagram next moves on the flip chart, and call a planning meeting (on the clock).

Cross Roads

....

- Select eight players.

- Have each player stand on a space, facing the center, leaving the center space open.

- Players must cross to the other side of the road.

Legal Moves

- A player may move into an empty space in front of him or her.

- A player may move around a person who is facing him or her into an empty space.

- Only one player may move at a time.

Illegal Moves

- A player may not move backward.

- A player may not move around someone facing the same way as he or she is, that is, if the player would be looking at the other person's back prior to the move.

- Two players may not move at the same time.

- Two players cannot occupy the same space at the same time.

- No player may step off of game space.

Duel Identity

● ●

● **PURPOSE**

- To learn about and interact with fellow players.

- To practice questioning techniques.

- To address the question of trust when interacting with another team or with fellow team members.

- To focus on methods of data verification when involved in problem solving.

● **TIME**

Thirty-five minutes.

● **PLAYERS**

Twelve or more.

● **SUPPLIES**

- An overhead transparency or newsprint flip-chart page of the Player Instructions for Duel Identity, prepared in advance by the facilitator.

- An overhead projector (if using a transparency).

- A newsprint flip chart and felt-tipped markers for each team.

- Two identical game sheets, made on newsprint flip-chart paper, prepared in advance by the facilitator. (Two Sample Game Sheets are provided at the end of this game, along with a Sample Characteristics Sheet that you can use to create your own game sheets.)

● STEPS

1. Divide the group into two teams. Have each team meet at one of the flip charts. Give each team paper, pencils, and felt-tipped markers.

2. Define the task: "This game is played in two rounds. Both teams have identical game sheets. Your first team task is to have team members sign for characteristics that apply to them, signing for as many total characteristics as possible. You only need one signature per characteristic. You will have twelve minutes for this task."

3. Display the Player Instructions, and begin Round 1.

4. After twelve minutes call time.

5. Define the second task: "Now you must go back to your game sheet and sign someone's name for three characteristics that do *not* apply to any member of your team. You will have three minutes for this task."

6. After three minutes call time. Award 1 point for every characteristic signed for on each team's game sheet (whether possessed by a member of the team or not). Post the scores.

7. Define the task for Round 2: "Teams will trade game sheets. You will have seven minutes to review the other team's game sheet and select the three signatures you believe are bogus, that is, the person does not possess that characteristic. Do not talk with your opponents except to verify a player or signature."

8. Start Round 2. After seven minutes call time.

9. Ask teams whether they would like to question a member of the opposing team about his or her qualifications. The rules for questioning are as follows:

a. You may *not* directly ask a player if he or she is qualified.

b. You may ask only two questions of any opposing player.

c. The person must answer the question in three words or less.

10. After the questioning period, have each team identify the three players on the opposing team who have claimed a characteristic they do not possess.

11. Award points as follows:

    a. Correct guess = 10 points

    b. Incorrect guess = minus 5 points

12. Tally the scores from both rounds. The team with the most points wins.

● FACILITATOR NOTES

- This is a suitable game to play as an icebreaker when working with either one team or two teams that interact in the workplace. This game will help all the players learn something about others that they did not know before. If you are familiar with the Johari Window (Luft, 1969), then you will see that this game enlarges the Arena, making communication a bit more productive.

- This game also surfaces the issue of trust—a major issue when people are dealing with one another for the first time. When dealing with others, either other team members or another team, the following question is on all participants' minds in some fashion: "Can these people be trusted?" Another way to ask that question is: "Will these people help me or hurt me?"

  The only way trust can be developed is by people working together and fulfilling the promises they have made. You can talk about trust until the cows come home, but that will not produce more trust. What produces trust is Person A telling Person B, "I will do this," and then doing it. When A does what he or she has promised to do, then B has some hard data about A's trustworthiness.

  When people meet for the first time, trust is usually an open question unless someone has been hurt so much in the past that he or she automatically mistrusts everyone new. However, concerns about trust are never expressed openly. B will usually ask C whether A can be trusted, rather than asking A directly.

  Trust is built when people live up to their promises. That produces behavioral evidence. It is therefore a good practice to promise only what one can deliver and no more. If someone is not sure whether he or she can deliver, it is better to say, "I will attempt to deliver this, but I have some doubts about my ability to be successful because of the barriers I have to overcome." This shows the other person not only that you tell the truth, but gives him or her the opportunity to ask you the kind of help you need to deliver on your promise.

If trust is broken, the only way to fix it is to have the people involved interact at some basic level and then slowly build trust back to a level that allows for productive working relationships.

This game is not meant to produce drastic changes in a team. Rather it allows a team or interacting teams to address the issue of trust before mistrust begins to interfere with their operations. Some of the outcomes to this game could be answers to such questions as:

How do we know when someone can be trusted?

What behaviors produce trust?

What behaviors produce mistrust?

What can we do to keep trust intact?

If trust is violated, what will the consequences be?

What can we do to rebuild trust?

Trust can be built between individuals and between teams if they have answers to these questions early in their relationship.

- Questioning skills. This game can be useful in helping team members learn how to use questions when they are involved in gathering data for problem solving. For example, members can practice open-ended questioning.

● CUSTOMIZING DUEL IDENTITY

Regarding Group Size

- For smaller groups use a smaller number of characteristics and/or reduce the number of mistaken identities to one or two.

- For groups larger than forty, divide participants into two sets of teams and post additional game sheets. Larger groups may require additional facilitators.

Regarding Time

- Shorten or lengthen time for each round of play.

- Expand or contract the number of characteristics.

Regarding Focus of the Task

- Change characteristics on the game sheets to suit your audience. A sample list of characteristics is provided.

- Use self-sticking notes to sign and attach them to appropriate characteristics, which allows you to use the same game sheets again.

- Introduce a module on questioning techniques. Use the questioning period as preparation for interviews or inquiries by changing the questioning procedure, such as setting a time limit or allowing questions that can only be answered "yes" or "no."

Regarding Scoring

- Change the point system for Round 2 to +15 points for a correct guess and no points for an incorrect guess.

- Charge teams 2 points for each question they ask of opposing players.

Reference

Luft, J. (1969). *Of human interaction.* Palo Alto, CA: National Press.

Duel Identity

- Divide into two teams.

- Round One

  First Task: Sign for all characteristics that apply to at least one of your team members.

  Second Task: Sign for three additional characteristics that do not apply to a member of your team.

- Receive 1 point for every signature.

- Round Two

  Identify the three signatures from your opponents' game sheet that do NOT apply to a member of their team.

- Receive 10 points for each correct guess and –5 points for each incorrect guess.

Duel Identity

....

Use this sheet to create your own list of items.

- Plays [musical instrument]

- Plays [specific sport or activity, such as ping pong]

- Owns or drives [car, truck, motorcycle, jet ski]

- Married for [number of years]

- Collects [stamps, coins, dolls, glassware]

- Enjoys [painting, potting, sculpting, reading, gardening]

- Dances [ballroom, tap, ballet, square]

- Writes [music, poetry, prose]

- Owns [tuxedo, fur coat, red carpet, velvet hat]

- Likes to go [shopping, scuba diving, camping, sailing]

- Likes to cook [French, Italian, Chinese]

- Has lived in [specific city, state, or country]

- Has five or more [children, grandchildren, sisters, brothers]

- Owns a [jacuzzi, sauna, swimming pool, sports car]

- Has seen [play, ballet, rock group, famous place]

- Is a [car, boat, hunting, specific sport] enthusiast

- Served in the [Army, Navy, Peace Corps]

- Has a [web page, airplane, boat]

- Is fluent in [French, Spanish, Russian, Japanese]

- Has published [book, professional article, poetry]

- Has [done community work, donated blood, served on bond drives]

- Owns a [Persian cat, ferret, Malamute]

- Is a certified [pilot, computer operator, nurse, meeting planner]

- Attends [concerts, auto races, wrestling matches, football games]

- Met a spouse [in high school, on a blind date, in church, at work]

- Can [ride horses, skateboard, hang glide, pilot a plane]

- Shops from [L.L. Bean, Orvis, Lands' End] catalog

- Subscribes to [*Time, Reader's Digest, Modern Maturity*]

- Owns [name of video, record, or book]

- Has been on [radio, television, stage]

Duel Identity

1. Jogs over ten miles per week.
2. Plays the ukelele.
3. Has his or her own web page.
4. Can use chopsticks.
5. Took ballet or tap.
6. Lived in California for over ten years.
7. Rides a motorcycle.
8. Is licensed to fly an airplane.
9. Has five or more children.
10. Owns a snake.
11. Has had a root canal.
12. Has seen the opera *Carmen*.
13. Is an avid skier.
14. Have been on television.
15. Has video of child's first birthday.
16. Does not have cable television.
17. Can skateboard.
18. Can tie a bow tie.

Jossey-Bass/Pfeiffer

Duel Identity

Sings in a choir	Jogs ten miles a week	Reads two books a week	Is a par 80 golfer	Owns an oriental rug	Collects coins
Owns a tuxedo	Is an avid skier	Uses chopsticks	Cans vegetables	Has his or her own web page	Keeps a diary
Makes pots	Once met Elvis	Rides a motorcycle	Plays the ukelele	Drives a Porsche	Owns a fur coat
Owns a condo	Is fluent in two languages	Took ballet or tap	Has three or more grand-children	Has had a root canal	Makes jewelry
Makes rugs	Owns a French poodle	Has seen opera Carmen	Ice skates	Is a licensed pilot	Married less than one year
Can tie a bow tie	Can dance the samba	Was born in Canada	Is a twin	Lived in Wyoming	Is an only child

High Five

. . . .

● PURPOSE

- To identify important team characteristics.

- To transition to the subject of teams.

- To focus on good team skills.

● TIME

Twenty-five minutes.

● PLAYERS

Ten or more.

● SUPPLIES

- An overhead transparency or newsprint flip-chart page of the Player Instructions for High Five, prepared in advance by the facilitator.

- A newsprint flip chart and felt-tipped markers for each team.

- A list of twenty characteristics of a well-functioning team, with examples, if possible, prepared in advance by the facilitator on newsprint or an overhead transparency.

- An overhead projector (if using transparencies).

- Paper and pencils for teams.

- Masking tape.

● STEPS

1. Divide the group into teams of four to six players. Have each team meet at its own table.

2. Distribute paper and pencils and one sheet of newsprint paper and felt-tipped markers to each team.

3. Define the task: "Each team has five minutes to identify the five most important characteristics describing a well-functioning team."

4. Post the Player Instructions, and begin the game.

5. Call time at the end of five minutes and have each team post its list of five characteristics.

6. Post your own list of twenty characteristics.

7. Award 1 point for every characteristic on a team's list that matches one from your list.

8. Total each team's points. Declare the team with the most points the winner.

● FACILITATOR NOTES

- This game is intended as a way to focus attention on the question: "What makes an effective team?" High Five can be used at the start of a team-building session, as a transition from another topic to the topic of team building, or as an energizer after lunch.

- This game is normative in the sense that the facilitator establishes twenty important characteristics that are used as a standard against which the lists developed by the teams will be judged. It will take the groups a little longer to do this exercise because not only are they trying to come up with five characteristics, but they are trying to match your list in order to receive points.

- The discrepancy between what you write down and what the participants write down will provide good data for a discussion about the positive characteristics of a team. Time can be profitably spent discussing each characteristic and why it is important.

- You will gain insight into the thinking of the participants through the characteristics that they post. Find out why the participants think the characteristics they post that are not on your list are important. Some of the positive characteristics that the participants post may stem from negative experiences they have had on a team, so they list characteristics they believe would prevent that experience from happening again.

- This game focuses on the positives of being part of a team, allowing participants to focus on the benefits of being a good team, rather than on negative experiences in the past. It can keep the session from becoming bogged down with "horror stories" from the participants' past.

● CUSTOMIZING HIGH FIVE

Regarding Group Size

- For smaller groups, have individual players develop lists of three characteristics and compare them with other players' lists.

Regarding Time

- Shorten or lengthen rounds of play, as needed.

Regarding the Focus of the Task

- Have each team post the five most important characteristics on flip-chart paper. Post the sheets and have players vote for the best set of characteristics other than their own.

Regarding Scoring

- To encourage "team power," award bonus points for every characteristic that is identified by another team. This can be done in one of two ways:

  Award 3 points to each team for each characteristic they identify that is also identified by another team.

  Award 1 point to each team for each characteristic identified by one other team; 2 points for each characteristic identified by two other teams, etc.

High Five

....

- Divide into teams.

- List the five most important characteristics of a well-functioning team.

- Post your list of five characteristics.

- Compare your list against the facilitator's list.

- Receive 1 point for each item on your list that matches an item on the facilitator's list.

Line Up

· ·

● **PURPOSE**

- To demonstrate the communication and cooperation required for a whole team project.

- To practice problem-solving skills.

- To practice coaching skills.

- To practice team learning.

● **TIME**

Thirty minutes.

● **PLAYERS**

Ten or more.

● **SUPPLIES**

- An overhead transparency or newsprint flip-chart page of the Player Instructions for Line Up, prepared in advance by the facilitator.

- An overhead transparency or newsprint flip-chart page of the final sequence, as shown in Step 5, prepared in advance by the facilitator.

- An overhead projector (if using transparencies).

- A newsprint flip chart and felt-tipped markers.

- Masking tape.

- One set of eight player cards, prepared in advance by the facilitator. The cards should be made from 8½" x 11" index stock. Each card should be marked on both sides with a single digit, from 1 to 8.

● STEPS

1. Form teams of ten or more players.

2. Create a players' grid as follows: Using masking tape, outline a six-foot square on the floor. Divide this square into two-foot sections, creating a 3 by 3 grid.

3. Have the team select eight players to fill the grid. Each player will stand in one space of the grid, leaving the center space free. Two of the other players will act as "coach" and "recorder."

   a. The recorder's role is to document the moves of the team members. This record can be used during team planning and debriefing.

   b. The coach's role is to help the team plan, coordinate, and execute the moves.

4. Distribute a set of player cards to the players standing in the grid, as shown.

8	7	6
5		4
3	2	1

5. Define the task: "The team members will have fifteen minutes to rearrange themselves into the final sequence, as shown on the flip chart or overhead."

1	2	3
4		5
6	7	8

6. Explain the following rules of movement.

   a. A player may only move into an open space.

   b. A player may only move horizontally or vertically. No diagonal moves are allowed.

   c. A player may not move outside of the grid.

6. Post the Player Instructions and final grid configuration, and start the game.

7. Call time at the end of fifteen minutes or when the team has achieved the final sequence.

● SAMPLE ROUND OF PLAY AND SOLUTION

1. Players line up in the start sequence:

8	7	6
5		4
3	2	1

2. Move 1: Player 7 moves to center space to start play.

8	↓	6
5	7	4
3	2	1

3. Move 2: All outer numbers move clockwise one space . . .

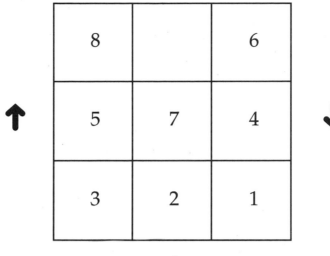

until they line up:

1	2	3
4	7	5
6		8

4. Move 3: Player 7 moves from center to bottom middle space.

1	2	3
4	↓	5
6	7	8

5. This completes player moves. The team has completed its line up.

- Line Up is a game that will pep up the participants right after lunch. It requires people to move around and to be actively engaged in solving a problem.

- One essential skill for a team leader is the ability to coach, that is, to get the team from where it is to where it wants to go. Line Up provides practice in being a team coach.

  Some of the behaviors the coach will have to deal with are people who move on their own (the highly motivated), people who do not listen (because they are bored or frustrated or want to try their own methods), and people who just want to end the game (inability to stick with a complicated problem). Watch how the coach manages these behaviors. Are the behaviors ignored? Does the team agree to do something different the next time the behaviors surface?

  One sign to watch for is how the team's behavior impacts the coach. Studies have shown that when a person or group moves closer to accomplishing its goal it becomes more energized. The closer they come to the end, the more energy you will find in the group. Some things to watch for include: What energizes the coach, what impact the coach's energy has on the team, and the impact the team's energy has on the coach.

  The coach may also be impacted if the team is not doing well. People may not be paying attention, some may have dropped out, and some may start a side show. Watch for how the coach handles these situations. If the team's energy is low, what does that do to the coach? What behaviors does the coach use to combat low team energy?

  An interesting question to discuss when the team has some members who are not really participating is, "What does [the behavior] mean for membership on a team?" Discuss whether people who do not want to be on a team or a certain project should be assigned to it anyway.

  As a side benefit of looking at the coach's role in some depth, you can develop a list of behaviors that are signs of effective coaching and signs of ineffective coaching.

- Another common occurrence in team meetings is that the same topic is brought up after it has already been discussed. This happens because people think in a linear fashion and may forget what happened earlier. One purpose of team learning is to capture knowledge that is useful to the team, to capture lessons the team has already learned so that it does not have to relearn them.

This function can be fulfilled by having a recorder keep track of what the team has learned and let the members know when they are ignoring a lesson already learned. The recorder can serve as the team memory. It may be enlightening for a team to see how its performance is improved by having someone who can remind members when they are forgetting a previous lesson.

- A common complaint heard from team members is that they have to attend meetings that do not concern them. The roles of coach and recorder serve to highlight how team members can contribute, even when they are not directly involved in solving a problem.

● CUSTOMIZING LINE UP

Regarding Group Size

- This game requires at least eight players to act as one team, ten if you wish to use a coach and a recorder.

- Use additional game grids for larger groups, but allow for additional time to discuss and process the game.

- Use one grid and have teams take turns rearranging different, and progressively more challenging, Line Up sequences.

Regarding Time

- Shorten or lengthen time for a round of play.

Regarding Focus of the Task

- Allow for one or more team planning meetings. The planning time may, or may not, be deducted from the overall time.

- Divide the eight players into two teams and give one cards with the letter "X" and the other cards with the letter "O." Have players form any different sequence or try to get three "X" or "O" cards in a row, as in Tic-Tac-Toe.

Line Up

··

- Select eight players per team.

- Place players in the spaces of the grid, leaving the center space free.

- Each player receives a number card.

- Players must rearrange into a new numerical "line up" that matches the posted grid.

- Players may move ONLY:

  Into an open space

  One space at a time

  Horizontally or vertically on grid

- Players may NOT:

  Move diagonally

  Move outside the grid

  Share a space

Match Point

· ·

● PURPOSE

- To demonstrate realistic goal setting.

- To explore the power of expectations.

● TIME

Twenty-five minutes.

● PLAYERS

Six or more.

● SUPPLIES

- An overhead transparency or newsprint flip-chart page of the Player Instructions for Match Point, prepared in advance by the facilitator.

- An overhead transparency or newsprint flip-chart page of the Scoring Matrix for Match Point, prepared in advance by the facilitator.

- An overhead projector (if using transparencies).

- A newsprint flip chart and felt-tipped markers.

- One set of Question Sheets for Match Point for each team, prepared in advance by the facilitator. (*Note:* Each Question Sheet consists of seven questions. Each round of play requires one Question Sheet. The number of Question Sheets prepared is at the discretion of the facilitator. A sample sheet, with answers, is provided at the end of this game.)

- Paper and pencils for each participant.

● STEPS

1. Divide the group into teams of four to six players each.

2. Distribute paper and pencils to each person.

3. Define the task: "This game is played in rounds. Each round consists of your team's estimating how many correct answers you will provide for sets of seven questions and then attempting to answer the questions. After you have answered the questions, your score will be determined by the Scoring Matrix. You will have five minutes to answer each set of questions."

4. Display the Player Instructions and the Scoring Matrix for Match Point. Distribute one set of Question Sheets for Match Point to each team, and start the game.

5. After five minutes, call time. Poll the teams as to their answers on each of the questions. Provide and discuss the correct answers, as needed.

6. Help the participants to compute their scores according to the Scoring Matrix.

7. Record each team's points on a newsprint flip chart.

8. Continue each round of play in the same manner, for as many rounds or for as long as is appropriate. At the end of Match Point, declare the team with the most points the winner.

● SCORING EXAMPLE

1. For Round 1.

   a. Team A estimates it will provide four correct answers.

   b. Team B estimates it will provide seven correct answers.

   c. Team C estimates it will provide six correct answers.

2. In the first round, Team A provided six correct answers.

    a. Team A exceeded its estimate of four.

    b. Team A receives 4 x 3 points, plus 1 point for each correct response above four, for a total of 14 points.

3. In the first round, Team B provided six correct answers.

    a. Team B did *not* match its estimate of seven.

    b. Team B receives 2 points for each correct answer, for a total of 12 points.

4. In the first round, Team C provided six correct answers.

    a. Team C matched its estimate of six.

    b. Team C receives 6 x 3, plus 7 bonus points, for a total of 25 points.

● FACILITATOR NOTES

- It is not uncommon for individuals to be optimistic in setting their goals, then give many reasons why they could not do it if they do not reach the goals they set. This unfounded optimism is different from setting goals that are a stretch and realizing from the start that you will need to expend extra effort to accomplish your goals.

  It is also not uncommon for individuals to set their goals low, knowing that they can exceed them. They then expect a reward for exceeding their low goals.

  Both situations interfere with a rational approach to managing a team's work. The team leader never knows whether the team will meet its goals, as the way the goals are set renders them worthless for planning the work.

  This game encourages people to be realistic in setting their goals by awarding bonus points for teams that meet their goals exactly. Once the teams understand this, your job as facilitator will be to encourage the teams to talk about how they set goals now and how they might change that process, based on their experience during this game.

- Match Point also highlights how expectations can affect energy levels. If someone sets unrealistically high goals he or she may not expend a lot of energy trying to meet them because the goals were unrealistic in the first place. The person relies on luck and does not dig deeper for extra energy needed.

If someone has goals lower than he or she knows can be achieved, that person's energy level will also be low and he or she will experience no sense of satisfaction for a job well done.

Only those people who set realistic goals and meet them feel a sense of accomplishment and an extra burst of energy.

- Use the Team Group Process Sheet from RAT Race on page 166 to allow the teams to process their performance between rounds.

- Match Point can also be used to discuss setting goals during the performance appraisal process for the team or for individual members of the team.

- If you have chat room and e-mail capability, you can play Match Point over the Internet. Set up mail groups and prepare the questions ahead of time to speed up the process. Each team needs to have its own chat room where team members can discuss the answers to the questions.

● CUSTOMIZING MATCH POINT

Regarding Group Size

- Divide larger groups into two or more teams.

- Use additional question sheets for larger groups. Allow more time to discuss and process the items.

Regarding Time

- Adjust the time allowed for answers, depending on the complexity of the questions.

- Vary the number of rounds to match the available time.

Regarding Focus of the Task

- Prepare case studies that have several examples that the teams must find. Have teams estimate how many examples they will be able to find.

- Use Match Point to prepare groups for goal setting during performance appraisal or strategic planning.

Regarding Scoring

- Increase or decrease the point bonus. This can be done before the game or as a change during game play, such as for the final round.

- Use different point combinations to change game dynamics, such as:

  Give 1 point for each correct response plus a 5-point bonus.

  Give 3 points for each correct response, plus an 11-point bonus.

- Use question sets of four, five, or six and keep the same scoring system.

- After time has been called, give teams the option of revising their original estimates for a penalty of 3 points, deducted from their final score.

Match Point

- Divide into teams.

- Estimate the number of questions you will answer correctly.

- Answer the questions.

- Compute your score according to the Scoring Matrix.

SCORING MATRIX FOR
Match Point

. . . .

Estimated Correct Answers	Actual Corrects Answers	Scoring	Bonus	Total Points
1	1	1 x 3	7	10
2	2	2 x 3	7	13
3	3	3 x 3	7	16
4	4	4 x 3	7	19
5	5	5 x 3	7	22
6	6	6 x 3	7	25
7	7	7 x 3	7	28

- If a team matches its estimate, it receives 3 points for each correct answer, plus 7 bonus points.

- If a team does NOT match its estimate, it receives 2 points for each correct answer, but no bonus points. (*Example:* A team estimates it will have 5 correct answers, but only has 4. Therefore, the team receives 2 points for each correct answer [4 x 2], but no bonus points, for a total of 8 points.)

- If a team exceeds its estimate, it receives 3 points for every correct answer and 1 point for each answer over Match Point, but no additional bonus points. (*Example:* A team estimates it will have 5 correct answers, but has 6. Therefore, the team receives 3 points for each correct answer [5 x 3], plus 1 point for its correct response over its estimate [1 x 1], for a total of 16 points.)

Match Point

....

1. On which team will there be more conflict?

   a. A team composed of average performers.

   b. A team composed of average and poor performers.

   c. A team composed of high performers.

   d. A team composed of poor performers.

   (Correct answer is c.)

2. On which team do members rarely if ever see one another?

   a. A cutting edge team.

   b. A team spirit team.

   c. A traditional team.

   d. A cyber-team.

   (Correct answer is d.)

3. What is the ideal number of people on a team?

   a. Two to five people.

   b. Four to nine people.

   c. Three to eight people.

   d. Three to twelve people.

   (Correct answer is b.)

4. von Bertalanffy says that:

   a. There are many ways to reach the same goal.

   b. Experienced people know the best way to reach a goal.

   c. The path to the goal must be explained to team members.

   d. There is only one way to reach a goal.

   (The correct answer is a.)

5. Conflict on a team is a sign of:

   a. Poor communication.

   b. Competing ideas.

   c. Team growth.

   d. Poor team leadership.

   (The correct answer is c.)

6. Which of the following is not a sign of a good team:

   a. Shared leadership.

   b. Mutual responsibility.

   c. Twelve to eighteen team members.

   d. Conscious authority.

   (The correct answer is c.)

7. An effective team should:

   a. Review its work procedures.

   b. Review its decision-making processes.

   c. Always question directions from the team leader.

   d. Assign responsibilities equally among team members.

   (Correct answers are a, b, and c.)

Name That Team

. . . .

● PURPOSE

- To identify what the participants believe are the characteristics of a good team.

- To transition from concerns outside the room to the topic under discussion.

- To transition from a previous topic to the topic of team building.

● TIME

Twenty minutes.

● PLAYERS

Sixteen or more.

● SUPPLIES

- An overhead transparency or newsprint flip-chart page of the Player Instructions for Name That Team, prepared in advance by the facilitator.

- An overhead projector (if using a transparency).

- A newsprint flip chart and felt-tipped markers.

- Masking tape.

- Paper and pencils for each participant.

1. Divide the group into teams of four to six players each. Have each team sit at a separate table.

2. Distribute one sheet of newsprint flip-chart paper, strips of masking tape, felt-tipped markers, and paper and pencils to each team.

3. Define the task for Round 1: "This game is played in three rounds. In the first round your team is to select a 'mystery' team that you think portrays many good team behaviors *or* many bad team behaviors. You are to develop a set of five to seven statements that describe this team's good or bad behavior. You will then post those statements on a flip chart. You will *not* post the mystery team's name. You have ten minutes to select the team, develop the statements, and write those statements (without identifying the team) on a sheet of newsprint. Here are two samples:

Sample 1: Effective Mystery Team

Team Name: 1998 New York Yankees

Team Behaviors: winning team tradition, skilled athletes, clear lines of authority, team members support one another, selfless, goal focused, excellent relations with the media

Sample 2: Ineffective Mystery Team

Team Name: H.M.S. Bounty

Team Behaviors: punitive ship captain, inflexible layers of management, one-way communication, no concern for well-being of lower team members, greedy top management, massive breakdown of lines of authority"

4. Display the Player Instructions, and start the game.

5. After ten minutes, call time. Instruct each team to give you a sheet of paper on which is listed (a) their own team name, (b) the five to seven team characteristics, and (c) the name of the mystery team.

6. Have each team post its newsprint list *without the mystery team name* on the wall.

7. Define the task for Round 2: "Each team has five minutes to try to guess the identity of the real or fictional mystery teams, based on the posted lists of statements."

8. After five minutes, call time and collect guesses from each team.

9. Award 7 points for each correct guess.

10. Post a separate list of the identities of all of the real or fictional mystery teams.

11. Define the task for Round 3: "Each team has three minutes to match the identity of the real or fictional mystery teams described with the list of team names just posted."

12. After three minutes, call time and collect the list of matches.

13. Award 3 points for each correct match.

14. Tally the final score. The team with the most points wins.

15. Have the winning team select one of the mystery teams described and explain to the class what can be learned about team building from the team they selected.

● FACILITATOR NOTES

- This game is an icebreaker that can be used to help participants to start focusing on the concept of team building.

- Name That Team helps participants to begin thinking about the qualities of an effective team and helps them to make the transition from what is happening outside the room to the topic being discussed.

- Name That Team can also be used to transition from a previous topic into the topic of team building.

- Leave the lists posted in the room. As you talk about various aspects of team building, go back to the lists and show where the topic fits in one or more of the team attributes developed by the participants.

- Name That Team can also be played with a cyber team that has access to e-mail and a conference area. Each team can place its attributes in a conference topic area and the other teams can attempt to guess the names. You could then go to a chat room and have the winning team select one of the teams described and explain to the group what can be learned about team building from the team they selected.

- Once the group has spent time talking about other teams, you can ask them to analyze their own behavior while playing this game. Ask:

What good qualities that were posted about a mystery team did you find present in your own team as you played this game?

What could you do as a team to make sure your good practices are used again the next time you work as a team?

What bad qualities that were posted about a mystery team did you find present in your team as you played this game?

Did you engage in those bad practices intentionally? Why do you think they happened?

What could you do as a team to make sure your bad practices do not surface the next time you work together as a team?

● CUSTOMIZING NAME THAT TEAM

Regarding Group Size

- For smaller groups, divide into only two teams.

Regarding Time

- Shorten or lengthen rounds of play, as needed.

Regarding Scoring

- For scoring in Round 2, award 7 points to *both* teams—the team that correctly guessed the mystery team and the team that developed the list of behaviors. This will encourage teams to use the better behaviors of their own mystery teams.

Regarding the Focus of the Task

- Prepare lists of teams with supporting behaviors in advance. Have teams randomly select a team from the list, then develop five more behaviors. Have teams list the ten behaviors on a flip chart and present them to the rest of the group. Have other teams then select the five most important behaviors. The presenting team receives 3 points for each one of its characteristics that are selected.

Jossey-Bass/Pfeiffer

Name That Team

· ·

- *Round 1.* Select a well-known team and list five to seven behaviors (either productive or not productive) of that team.

- *Round 2.* Guess the identities of others' mystery teams.

- Receive 7 points for each correct guess.

- *Round 3.* Match the list of mystery team names to the lists of mystery team behaviors.

- Receive 3 points for each positive match.

- Total your team's final score.

Norman Says!

● ●

● PURPOSE

- To explore the impact of team norms on team members' behavior.

- To explore the impact of norms on problem solving and decision making in the team.

- To explore the impact of norms on team communication.

- To develop guidelines for communicating about team norms.

● TIME

Fifteen minutes.

● PLAYERS

Twelve or more.

● SUPPLIES

- An overhead transparency or newsprint flip-chart page of the Player Instructions for Norman Says!, prepared in advance by the facilitator.

- An overhead projector (if using a transparency).

- A newsprint flip-chart sheet for each team.

- A flip chart and felt-tipped markers.

- A set of problem statements, with separate behavioral guidelines, prepared in advance by the facilitator.

- A large envelope or folder for each team.

- Paper and pencils for participants.

- Masking tape.

● STEPS

1. Divide the group into teams of four to six players. Have each team meet at its own table.

2. Copy enough problem statements for each member of the team and then write a different behavioral guideline on each sheet. Seal the sheets inside an envelope and distribute one envelope to each team, along with a sheet of newsprint and markers. (*Note:* Each sheet should contain the same problem statement, plus a different behavioral guideline for each person, as shown in the sample below. Additional Sample Behavioral Guidelines are given at the end of this activity.)

Sample Problem Statement: "During the last management audit, your office was cited for not providing a yearly figure for 'expendable' office supplies, such as paper, pencils, pens, tape, paper clips, toner, and so on. Your team must estimate this expense item for the next fiscal year's budget." (If you use this problem statement, supply each team with a copy of an office supply catalog.)

Sample Behavioral Guideline: "You think some other department should be responsible for mundane items, such as office supplies, and doodle or look out the window when the issue comes up."

3. Instruct participants to memorize the behavioral guideline on the sheet they receive and keep it confidential during game play.

4. Define the task: "Each team has fifteen minutes to solve the problem statement in the sealed envelopes it received. While solving the problem, each team member must abide by the behavioral guideline listed on the sheet that he or she received."

5. Post the Player Instructions, and begin the game.

6. Call time at the end of fifteen minutes and have each team post its solution on the newsprint paper.

7. Post solution(s) to the problem statement if appropriate.

8. Award 5 points to each correct problem solution, as appropriate.

● FACILITATOR NOTES

- Norman Says! explores the concept of norms and the effect of those norms on team behavior and communication. A norm is defined in Webster's as "a standard of conduct that must or should be followed." When norms can be discussed, they usually become rules, regulations, procedures, or performance expectations. Open norms are not the major concern of this game, but rather the unspoken expectations that people have of one another, as illustrated in the sample case below.

  A Sample Case: A supervisor approaches a manager to ask how the manager views the performance of Employee A. The manager says he thinks Employee A does very good work and is a reliable employee. The supervisor then asks, "Well, if that is so, then why don't you invite him to more of the meetings? You always talk to me about his projects, whereas with some of my other staff, you call them in to talk about their projects directly."

  The manager squirms a little bit in his seat and says, "Well, do you really want to know?" The supervisor nods. At that point the manager stands up and closes the door. He says, "You have to promise me that if I tell you the problem I will not have to meet with Employee A to discuss it." The supervisor agrees. The manager then tells the supervisor that he cannot stand the ties that Employee A wears, so he does not invite Employee A to meetings.

  The supervisor is dumbfounded. He asks, "What kind of ties should he wear?"

  The manager replies, "More traditional ties, such as plain blue, red, or even sophisticated striped ties."

  So the supervisor relays this information to Employee A. After they both have a good time trashing the manager, Employee A buys a couple of conservative clip-on ties. Whenever he is near the manager's office, he takes off his tie and replaces it with one of the conservative clip-ons. Within three months Employee A is being invited to meetings with the manager.

  Ridiculous? Probably. However, there are behaviors going on in your team or organization that stem from such unspoken norms. The good news about this particular scenario is that the manager was willing to talk about it. Once the norm became public, changes could be made to meet his expectations. In this scenario the decision was up to Employee A as to whether he would change his behavior. Much worse are cases in which the norms are not spoken, but still affect peoples' attitudes and behavior toward one another.

- Argyris and Schon (1996) talk about "secondary inhibitory loops" to organizational learning. They say that not only are unspoken norms not discussed, but that their not being discussable is also not discussed.

Norman Says! is designed to alert team members about their unspoken norms and how they are impacting team performance and productivity. Then teams can develop procedures for discussing unspoken norms and resolving related issues.

A Sample Case: A team leader hated the word "problem." If someone mentioned that there was a problem, she would refuse to listen. Over time a norm developed that problems were not to be discussed. Of course, employees were upset that they could not discuss problems, and this norm adversely affected the productivity of the unit. Through the help of an outside facilitator the team was eventually able to discuss this problem. Team members learned that what the team leader actually did not like was when people would dump their problems in a meeting and then do nothing about them.

The end result was that the team leader agreed to listen to problems as long as the employee(s) presenting the problem also presented some solutions. She also asked that the solutions be prioritized. The employees stopped talking about problems and began talking about "opportunities for growth and development." So open discussion of the norm resulted in an increase of productivity.

- Some questions specific to Norman Says! follow:

How did you feel about acting out the behavior required of you to illustrate the norm?

Did you act out the behavior?

a. If so, why did you do it?

b. If not, why did you not do it?

For those who did not use the behavior, could anything have changed that would have enabled you to use it?

a. If yes, what would have to have changed?

b. Is there a reason you did not ask for that change?

What prevented you from discussing how you felt about your task with the facilitator or the whole group?

Are you ever asked to do something at work that makes you feel the same way?

What do you do?

What would you like to do? Why can't you do it?

What would have to change so that you could discuss how you feel about what you are asked to do?

How can you prevent unspoken norms from becoming established on your team?

● CUSTOMIZING NORMAN SAYS!

Regarding Group Size

- Divide smaller groups into two teams.
- Use additional sets of problem statements and behavioral guidelines for larger groups. Allow for more time to discuss and process.

Regarding Time

- Shorten or lengthen rounds of play, as needed.

Regarding the Focus of the Task

- Allow for a break in play for questions and answers about the "behavioral guidelines." Guide discussion about the value of behavioral norms in the formation of a team.

Regarding Scoring

- Award bonus points for completing the project in the shortest time.
- Award bonus points for teams appropriately dealing with behavioral guidelines.

References

Argyris, C., & Schon, D. (1996). *Organizational learning II.* Reading, MA: Addison-Wesley.
Neufeldt, V. (Ed.). (1988). *Webster's new world dictionary of the American English* (3rd college ed.) New York: Simon and Schuster.

Norman Says!

....

- Divide into teams.

- Receive sealed problem statement and guidelines for behavior.

- Solve your problem statement as a team.

SAMPLE BEHAVIORAL GUIDELINES FOR
Norman Says!

....

- You dislike the color red and do not talk to people wearing red unless you cannot avoid it.

- You frown every time someone mentions the word "problem" because you think the person is trying to avoid responsibility.

- You dislike people who write with pencils and always find things wrong with documents written in pencil.

- You dislike people who have the answer to everything. As a result you do not participate when someone tries to dominate a discussion and you do not support the decision made.

- You dislike people who whine. You think that is childish behavior. When they start whining you sigh loudly.

- You tend to shake your head in disapproval when you see someone fidget or bite nails because you see this as a sign of weakness.

- You feel that other team members try to blame you for everything. Whenever someone asks any questions about your input, ask why he or she is picking on you.

- You do not like people who do not take on their fair share of the workload. As a result, you always squint and stare at anyone who says, "No."

- You dislike vanity. As a result, you cannot look anyone in the eye who wears expensive jewelry or who smells of cologne or perfume.

- You do not tell people what you really think for fear of upsetting them.

- You are cynical of anyone who flaunts the "latest" studies or surveys when discussing business. Laugh aloud whenever someone mentions a survey, study, or any form of statistics.

Pass the Buck

· ·

● PURPOSE

- To learn how to handle multiple priorities.

- To practice planning team behavior for managing many priorities.

- To practice team cooperation.

● TIME

Fifteen minutes.

● PLAYERS

Six or more.

● SUPPLIES

- An overhead transparency or newsprint flip-chart page of the Player Instructions for Pass the Buck, prepared in advance by the facilitator.

- An overhead projector (if using a transparency).

- A newsprint flip chart and felt-tipped markers.

- One object for every member of a team. Objects for any one team should differ in weight and size and should be easily found around the office or home, such as the following:

Bag of potato chips or marshmallows

Balloon filled with air or water

Box of paper clips, roll of masking tape or duct tape

Child's batting helmet, hard hat, or baseball cap

Coffee mug, empty or half-filled with water

Empty egg carton

Empty one- or two-liter plastic bottle

Hard boiled or raw egg

Ping-pong ball, Nerf® ball, wadded paper ball, or tennis ball

Rolled newspaper, roll of paper towels or toilet paper

Small cushion or pillow

Tennis shoe, slipper, or rolled pair of socks

● STEPS

1. Divide the group into teams of six. Have each team form a circle.

2. Assign one participant as the "point," to indicate the beginning and end of each cycle.

3. Give each team an assortment of five or six objects.

4. Define the task: "You have one minute to pass this set of objects around the circle three times. Each time the last object passes the 'point' is one complete cycle. If you drop any object, you must start the whole process again.

   The game is scored as follows:

   a. If your team has successfully passed all of the objects past the 'point' three times in one minute, then your team earns 15 points.

   b. Each additional object passing the 'point' earns 1 point."

5. Post the Player Instructions, and begin the game.

6. Call time at the end of one minute.

7. Award the appropriate points.

● FACILITATOR NOTES

- Pass the Buck is a straightforward game. The focus is on behaviors or skills that were practiced in the game that can be transferred back to the workplace. Some sample questions that can be asked are:

  Did the different size and weight of objects make a difference in how you handled them?

  Do you handle every project at work the same way?

  What behaviors produced good results for you?

  Can any of these behaviors be translated to your everyday work life?

- If desired, modify the Team Group Process Sheet from RAT Race (p. 166) to use between rounds of this game.

- This is a good game to play after lunch or when you need to energize a team.

● CUSTOMIZING PASS THE BUCK

Regarding Group Size

- For larger groups conduct several games simultaneously.

- Have smaller groups act as one team.

Regarding Time

- Shorten or lengthen time of play.

Regarding Scoring

- Compute the score to reflect the number of objects used during the round. A recommended formula is three times the number of objects, that is, five objects earn 15 points, six objects earn 18 points.

Regarding the Focus of the Task

- Play one round; establish a standard. Play a second round and establish a standard that is 20 percent higher. Play a third and fourth round at the higher standard. Debrief this in terms of "raising the bar" at work and in the industry.

- Play additional rounds, with previous winners receiving additional objects as a handicap.

- Assign each team one more object than the number of participants.

- Have teams estimate how many objects they can handle in the time period. The team with the highest number of successfully recycled objects wins.

- Require each player to hold a wadded paper ball in his or her right hand while passing other objects with the left hand.

PLAYER INSTRUCTIONS FOR
Pass the Buck

··

- **Divide into teams of six.**

- **Each team forms a circle.**

- **Your team receives several objects of different sizes and weight.**

- **Pass the objects around the circle three times in one minute. If you drop any object, start over.**

- **Points are awarded in this manner:**

  15 points for cycling objects three times in one minute.

  +1 point for each additional object that goes around the circle.

Power Tag

· ·

● **SPECIAL NOTE**

This game requires active physical interaction and should be closely monitored by the facilitator. Any participant who does not wish to take part should be allowed to sit out.

● **PURPOSE**

- To explore the concept of power in team relationships.

- To explore how individual survival needs surmount team cooperation when an individual feels threatened.

- To explore how competition affects the behavior of a team.

- To explore how gender and physical size impact a person's behavior during conflict.

● **TIME**

Twenty minutes, plus several hours for debriefing.

● **PLAYERS**

Eight or more.

● SUPPLIES

- An overhead transparency or newsprint flip-chart page of the Player Instructions for Power Tag, prepared in advance by the facilitator.

- An overhead projector (if using a transparency).

- A newsprint flip chart and felt-tipped markers.

- Strips of cloth, approximately 2" x 24," one for each player.

- One balloon for each player.

- Masking tape.

● STEPS

1. Have players attach cloth strips to one of their arms at the elbow with masking tape so that from 10 to 12 inches of cloth hangs down.

2. Distribute one balloon to each player. Have players inflate their balloons and hold them in the same hand as the arm with the "power tag." (If a strip is on the left elbow, the balloon is in the left hand.)

3. Have players place their other arms behind their backs. Tell them they may not use this arm during the game.

4. Define the task: "This is a game of survival. To survive you must be the last player with a 'power tag' still on your elbow. To play you move around the group and remove the tags from other players' elbows. Any player who loses his or her tag must sit down. You may defend yourself with the inflated balloon, but if you use your other arm to defend yourself you must sit down."

5. Post the Player Instructions, and begin the game.

6. Call time when only one player remains with a tag.

● FACILITATOR NOTES

- Power Tag is a very powerful game that can take from four to six hours to debrief. There should be at least three hours available to use to play this game. To cut this game short will create problems in a group.

- If a person decides not to play, respect the person's decision and do not force him or her or let the team force him or her to play. However, be sure to discuss how this relates to the person's behavior on the team in general.

- To debrief this game it is very important that you start with the questions in Chapter 3 under Establishing Reality on page 28. This game can affect people in many different ways, and therefore it is very important to establish what actually happened during the game before you go on to discuss what it means.

- Another way to discuss the meaning of what happened, after you have established the reality of what happened, is to ask, "How does this reflect your behavior back at work?" One team the author worked with spent three hours pointing out behavior at work that was mirrored in the play of the game and deciding how to change their behaviors at work.

- One of the purposes of this game is to discuss how power is distributed on a team, which is usually not an issue that a team wants to address. Use of power is perhaps *the* "closet issue" most difficult for a team to discuss.

- How power is used and distributed is at the root of many team disputes. Many team activities have to do with who uses power and how; who makes what decisions; how decisions are made; who develops the priorities; who distributes resources; who makes assignments; and who distributes rewards. If the team does not discuss these issues openly, then they will be in the background and cause the team to be dysfunctional.

- If a team does not discuss how a decision is going to be made, then it is very easy for someone who is working a hidden agenda to orchestrate the decision-making process. This can upset others on the team, but they may have no idea how it happened. If team members are aware of how power is used on their team, then it becomes difficult for someone to work a hidden agenda. The discussion of how power is used produces a more open environment.

- The result you want in this game is to have the team members discuss how they want to use power on various team issues. You may find yourself becoming a little more directive in your facilitating during this game, which may be necessary to keep the team on track as members engage in a lot of avoidance behavior.

- It is also useful during this game to explore how gender and size affect the play of the game. Did females tend to withdraw or were they the main attackers? Did large people try to overpower smaller people? Did males and females react differently to losing their power tags? Did anyone try to get a tag back in an underhanded way? Do events like this happen back at work?

- Because Western culture holds "individual achievement" as a cultural icon, building teams is not an easy task. Talk all you like about the benefits of cooperation and collaboration, but if an individual feels threatened, he or she will begin to act in a way that protects himself or herself. People try to protect themselves from others. How does that behavior play out during a team activity? What does it mean for the operation of a team if the team members really do want to cooperate and collaborate? If I feel threatened by other members of a team, am I really going to want to cooperate? How can a team achieve cooperation and collaboration without threatening the individual? In the Western world people usually will not put aside their self-interest just for the sake of the team. How does a team incorporate self-interest into its decision-making process?

● CUSTOMIZING POWER TAG

Regarding Group Size

- For larger groups, hold play-off rounds or single-elimination rounds with the order of teams being decided by the flip of a coin.

- For larger groups, create a circle of play and then have players draw straws for who goes into the circle first. Then, as each person is eliminated, another person can take his or her place.

Regarding the Focus of the Task

- Play more than one round. Discuss whether any additional strategies or alliances were established in the later rounds.

- Play additional rounds, with previous winners wearing one tag and other players wearing two tags.

- Create two- or three-player teams. If one player loses his or her tag, the entire team must sit down.

- Pit two intact work groups against one another and discuss the dynamics that relate to their behavior back on the job.

- Have the players hold the balloon between the arm with the "power tag" and their body. If a player loses the "power tag" or the balloon he or she must sit down.

PLAYER INSTRUCTIONS FOR
Power Tag

• **Receive "tag."**

• **Attach tag to elbow with tape.**

• **Receive balloon.**

• **Inflate balloon and hold it in same hand as tagged arm.**

• **Hold other arm behind your back. You may not use this arm during play.**

• **Remove tags from other players' arms. You may defend yourself with your balloon.**

• **Players who lose their tags must sit down.**

• **The last player with a tag wins.**

RAT Race

● ●

● **PURPOSE**

- To demonstrate critical thinking skills used in problem solving and decision making.

- To increase awareness of the power of assumptions.

- To learn how to increase team productivity and produce smooth working relationships.

- To increase awareness of how the external environment can influence internal team behavior.

- To demonstrate intra-team feedback procedures.

- To demonstrate the role of norms in performance.

- To practice goal setting.

- To practice meeting management.

● **TIME**

One and one-half to three hours.

● **PLAYERS**

Ten or more.

● SUPPLIES

- The following overhead transparencies or flip-chart sheets, prepared in advance by the facilitator:

  Introduction for RAT Race (Overhead 1)

  Example Sheet for RAT Race (Overhead 2)

  Objective for RAT Race (Overhead 3)

  Player Instructions for RAT Race (Overhead 4)

  Solutions for RAT Race (Overhead 5)

  Score Sheet for RAT Race (Overhead 6)

- An overhead projector (if using transparencies).

- A newsprint flip chart and felt-tipped markers.

- One sheet of newsprint paper per round per team for their Team Group Process Sheet.

- One set of twelve Game Sheets for RAT Race. Photocopy the sheets, which are provided at the end of this game, and cut them in half. Prepare up to six pages of each game sheet.

- One Individual Group Process Sheet for RAT Race per player per round. (A copy is provided at the end of this game.)

- A copy of the Team Group Process Sheet for RAT Race for each team.

- A transparency mask or piece of cardboard to allow parts of the transparencies to remain hidden.

- Paper and pencils for each player.

- Masking tape.

- A stopwatch (optional).

● STEPS

1. Divide the group into teams of four to six players. Have each team meet at a separate table.

2. Have each team pick a team name. Record each team's name on the score sheet.

3. Introduce the concept of RATs by showing Overhead 1, Introduction for RAT Race. Explain: "A RAT is a *Remote Association Test,* a series of three clue words that are associated by one linking word. The linking word can be associated by means of:

a. One-word combinations: firsthand

b. Hyphenated words: first-rate

c. Two-word combinations: first aid

4. Show Overhead 2, Example Sheet for RAT Race, and present the three examples of linking words that:

a. Fall in *front* of clue words.

b. Fall *behind* the clue words.

c. Fall in *front of or behind* the clue words.

5. Display Overhead 3, Objective for RAT Race: "To collect as many points as you can by successfully solving the assigned RATs within the given time."

6. Display Overhead 4, Player Instructions for RAT Race, and define the task: "Your team will receive a set of five RATs. You will have ninety seconds to solve all five RATs. If your team solves all five RATs, it will receive 13 points. If the team does *not* solve all five RATs, it will lose 8 points."

7. *Round 1.* Distribute one RATs game sheet to each team. Each team should receive a different version. (Each player on Team A receives one copy of Game Sheet 1, each player on Team B receives one copy of Game Sheet 2, and so on.)

8. After each player has a game sheet, begin the game.

9. Stop play at the end of ninety seconds. Collect one completed game sheet from each team, that is, one copy of completed Game Sheet 1 from Team A, one copy of completed Game Sheet 2 from Team B, etc.)

10. Using Overhead 5, Solutions for RAT Race, verify each set of RATs.

11. Record each team's score on Overhead 6, the Score Sheet for RAT Race, or use a newsprint flip chart.

12. Distribute one Individual Group Process Sheet for RAT Race to each player and ask everyone to fill out their sheets individually and then meet with the rest of their team to share their information with one another.

13. After five minutes, distribute a copy of the Team Group Process Sheet to each team and ask them to fill it out, based on their individual sheets.

14. Give each team a sheet of newsprint and markers so they can transfer what they have written onto a chart that everyone in the group can see.

15. After ten minutes, ask each team to share its findings with the rest of the group and ask participants whether they have any questions for one another.

16. *Round 2.* Distribute a different RAT Race game sheet to each team and proceed as before, again asking participants whether they have any questions of one another and giving them Team Group Process Sheets to fill out.

17. *Round 3.* Distribute another RAT Race game sheet to each team and play another round, again asking participants whether they have any questions and having them fill out Group Process Question Sheets, and then concluding the game.

● SCORING EXAMPLE

1. The group forms three teams of five players each: Teams A, B, and C.

2. The facilitator distributes copies of the Game Sheets for RAT Race.

   a. Team A receives five copies of Game Sheet 1.

   b. Team B receives five copies of Game Sheet 2.

   c. Team C receives five copies of Game Sheet 3.

3. The facilitator begins the game. After ninety seconds, all teams hand in one copy of their game sheets.

4. Team A offers the following solutions to Game Sheet 1:

Clue Words	Linking Word
civil, birthday, swim	suit
partner, night, movie	silent
plant, line, horse	[left blank]
bee, comb, moon	honey
twister, depressor, tied	tongue

5. Team A's linking words are compared to the linking words shown on the Solutions sheet.

   a. Team A listed only four linking words correctly.

   b. The correct linking word for the third set is "power."

   c. Team A receives minus 8 points.

6. Facilitator records –8 points under Team A, Round 1, on the Score Sheet.

7. Team B offers the following solutions to Game Sheet 2:

Clue Words	Linking Word
super, lone, movie	critic [incorrect solution]
sun, jet, television	set
cloth, coffee, conference	table
Yogi, teddy, grizzly	bear
heart, tooth, bitter	sweet

8. Team B's linking words are compared to the linking words on the Solutions sheet.

   a. Team B solved only four linking words correctly.

   b. "Critic" is not the linking word; "star" is the correct solution.

   c. Team B receives minus 8 points.

9. Facilitator records –8 points under Team B, Round 1, on the Score Sheet.

10. Team C offers the following solutions to Game Sheet 3:

Clue Words	Linking Word
bed, feature, date	double
bottle, crew, tie	neck
plant, doll, dream	house
big, square, ball	foot
cottage, cake, American	cheese

11. Team C's linking words are compared to the Solutions sheet (Overhead 5).

   a. Team C solved all five linking words correctly.

   b. Team C receives 13 points.

12. Facilitator records +13 points under Team C, Round 1 on the RAT Race Score Sheet.

● FACILITATOR NOTES

- Many groups misinterpret the objective of the game as win-lose. The objective does *not* specify a winner and a loser. It calls for teams to optimize their points. When the teams start to complain about the game, the best question to ask is: "What is your objective?" Most participants will have interpreted the objective as win-lose and not see the distinction between that and "Score as many points as you can."

- The scoring for RAT Race are purposely punitive. If every team could experience success in the first round, it would then be very difficult to see the value of team learning.

- When teams score points in the first or second round, their success often makes them resistant to change, even when they do not do as well in the subsequent rounds. The behavior of these teams provides a real-time example of dealing with resistance to change.

- The success of one team early in the game creates very interesting dynamics on the other teams, who seem to redouble their efforts or start blaming their lack of success on the difficulty of the words that they are assigned. The assumption that the rules themselves are right is reinforced by the early success of one team.

- It usually takes the other teams some time to discover that, just because the rules work for one team, it does not mean that the rules are good and should not be changed.

- When someone complains about the game, the best question to ask is: "What would you like to change or do differently?" Focus on what the participants did and why and on what they would like to change and why. This will give them a sense of ownership and empowerment, concepts that can translate back to the workplace.

- One of the goals of this game is to have the team members become aware that their assumptions can impact the team's success. However, questions about changing the game should come only from the teams. Do not suggest it yourself. If the group asks for a change in the rules, ask what rules they would like to change to enable them to meet the goal of the game. The players may want one or more of the following: more time, points for each correct solution, the whole group to act as one team, or teams to help one another.

- If the groups are encountering difficulty in solving all the RATs and have not asked for a change by the end of Round 2, suggest that the participants examine their assumptions about the game or look outside their group for changes that could help them accomplish their task. This leads to a discussion on where the greatest barriers to performance lie—within ourselves or outside the work group.

- If, during Round 3, no team has asked for a change in the rules, the frustration level may be very high. Ask the group, "What stands in the way of you improving your performance?" You may hear "the rules." Usually this is said very softly, as many participants are hesitant to challenge the instructor or "the rules." You have the option of ignoring the soft-spoken challenge or asking the person to repeat it so all can hear. You can then lead a discussion on why it took them so long to challenge the rules and how failure to challenge the rules in their everyday work may interfere with their productivity.

- A discussion about change will not be productive until the group is clear about the actual goal of the game. This game shows clearly how lack of clarity about goals can lead to wasted energy.

- The Individual Group Process Sheet helps the participants to look at their own behavior during the game and to spark dialogue among team members, rather than defensiveness.

- You may want to present information about team building prior to playing RAT Race. However, the authors have found that the debriefing is actually richer when initial information on teams and teamwork is not presented.

- In addition to the debriefing questions in Chapter Three, some additional questions that can help you process the learning from RAT Race follow:

  What behaviors you learned while playing RAT Race can be used productively back at work?

  How would you go about using these new behaviors?

  What can your group do to become a better team?

● CUSTOMIZING RAT RACE

Regarding Group Size

- Divide smaller groups into two teams.

- Use additional game sheets for larger groups and make sure that no two adjacent teams have the same game set.

Regarding Time

- Lengthen the time for each round of play. This is usually prompted by requests from the group to expand the time to two or more minutes.

- Allow additional time for groups to discuss their strategies before each round.

Regarding Focus of the Task

- Use two leaders to focus on the content and the process of the game.

    The Game Master focuses on the *content* of the game—conducting the game, sharing the answers, determining the score for each team, and leading any discussion about changes in the rules of play.

    The Facilitator focuses on the *process* of the game—helping the participants to look at their behavior during the play of RAT Race and to learn ways to improve their performance in groups or on teams.

- Allow all teams to vote on the validity of an answer when it is not on the Solution sheet. This provides an opportunity to discuss inter-group relations and issues of trust.

- Create your own RATs. First, select a linking word, such as "tear." Then, using a dictionary and other resources, develop the three clue words, such as "tear-jerker," "teardrop," and "tear gas."

- If one team completes its game sheet quickly, allow the members to assist other teams.

Regarding Scoring

- Allow teams to provide four of the five correct linking words for a score of 13 points.

- Change scoring to allow for only a certain number of positive points to be awarded for each correct linking word, with no penalty.

INTRODUCTION FOR
RAT Race

....

What Is a RAT?

A *remote association test* or "RAT" is a series of three clue words that are associated by one linking word. The linking word can be associated as part of a:

- One-word combination (*first*hand)

- Hyphenated word (*first*-rate)

- Two-word combination (*first* aid)

EXAMPLE SHEET FOR
RAT Race

....

Example 1

Find the appropriate linking word that can be placed in FRONT of each of the following clue words:

_____ check   _____ forest   _____ coat

acceptable solution: rain

rain check   rain forest   raincoat

Example 2

Find the appropriate linking word that can be placed BEHIND each of the following clue words:

voice _____   fan _____   air _____

acceptable solution: mail

voice mail   fan mail   air mail

Example 3

Find the appropriate linking word that can be placed IN FRONT OF OR BEHIND each of the following clue words:

_____ burns _____   _____ river _____   _____ arm _____

acceptable solution: side

sideburns   riverside   sidearm

OBJECTIVE FOR
RAT Race

• •

To collect as many points as you can by successfully solving the assigned RATs within the given time.

PLAYER INSTRUCTIONS FOR
RAT Race

· ·

- **Divide into teams.**

- **Round 1.**

  Solve the first set of five RATs.

- **Receive points:**

  +13 points for solving five RATs

  –8 points for NOT solving five RATs

- **Hold a team meeting.**

- **Play is the same for all rounds.**

SOLUTIONS FOR
RAT Race

....

Sheet 1   suit, silent, power, honey, tongue

Sheet 2   star, set, table, bear, sweet

Sheet 3   double, neck, house, foot, cheese

Sheet 4   French, big, team, high, love

Sheet 5   cold, break, sign, ground, free

Sheet 6   safety, key, message, size, middle

Sheet 7   run, off, human, apple, name

Sheet 8   silver, single, trap, battle, old

Sheet 9   machine, color, down or up, hand, pay

Sheet 10   salad, peace, point, box, fly

Sheet 11   news, door, pin, place, book

Sheet 12   fire, paint, chair, slow, party

SCORE SHEET FOR
RAT Race

	Team	Team	Team	Team	Team
Round 1					
Round 2					
Round 3					

Jossey-Bass/Pfeiffer

INDIVIDUAL GROUP PROCESS SHEET FOR
RAT Race

· ·

Name: _____ Round: _____

1. What did we do as a group that helped us reach our goal and that we should continue to do next time?

   • What should I personally continue to do?

2. What did we do as a group that hindered us in reaching our goals and that we should not do next time?

   • What did I personally do that I should not do next time?

3. What did we do as a group that helped us reach our goal and that we should do more of next time?

   • What should I do more of?

4. What did we as a group do that we should do less of next time?

   • What should I do less of next time?

5. What did we *not* do as a group that would be helpful if we did do it next time?

   • What should I start to do next time?

RAT Race

· ·

- After your team members have completed their Individual Group Process Sheets, review the following chart, and then draw it on the newsprint sheet that was distributed earlier.

Start	Stop
Continue	More of
	Less of

- Notice that categories correspond with the questions on your individual forms.

- Share your findings from your individual form with your team members and create a team report on the newsprint sheet.

- Select a member of your team to explain the team's report to the rest of the participants.

- Use this procedure for each round.

  You may find at some point that you no longer need to use your individual forms and can simply fill out this form for your team.

RAT Race

· ·

Your score for this round: _____

Directions: Find the best common linking word for each set of clues.

Clue Words			**Linking Words**
civil	birthday	swim	_____
partner	night	movie	_____
plant	line	horse	_____
bee	comb	moon	_____
twister	depressor	tied	_____

GAME SHEET 2 FOR

RAT Race

· ·

Your score for this round: _____

Directions: Find the best common linking word for each set of clues.

Clue Words			**Linking Words**
super	lone	movie	_____
sun	jet	television	_____
cloth	coffee	conference	_____
Yogi	teddy	grizzly	_____
heart	tooth	bitter	_____

RAT Race

. . . .

Your score for this round: _____

Directions: Find the best common linking word for each set of clues.

Clue Words			**Linking Words**
bed	feature	date	_____
bottle	crew	tie	_____
plant	doll	dream	_____
big	square	ball	_____
cottage	cake	American	_____

GAME SHEET 4 FOR

RAT Race

. . . .

Your score for this round: _____

Directions: Find the best common linking word for each set of clues.

Clue Words			**Linking Words**
toast	cuff	kiss	_____
bird	top	business	_____
baseball	player	building	_____
school	heels	chair	_____
letter	boat	puppy	_____

RAT Race

· ·

Your score for this round: _____

Directions: Find the best common linking word for each set of clues.

Clue Words			**Linking Words**
ice	head	war	_____
even	coffee	lucky	_____
stop	dollar	language	_____
hog	back	zero	_____
association	lance	duty	_____

RAT Race

· ·

Your score for this round: _____

Directions: Find the best common linking word for each set of clues.

Clue Words			**Linking Words**
net	pin	belt	_____
board	chain	low	_____
secret	mixed	center	_____
life	king	queen	_____
east	age	management	_____

RAT Race

· ·

Your score for this round: _____

Directions: Find the best common linking word for each set of clues.

Clue Words			**Linking Words**
end	way	down	_____
blast	duty	key	_____
being	super	rights	_____
cider	big	sauce	_____
brand	first	calling	_____

RAT Race

· ·

Your score for this round: _____

Directions: Find the best common linking word for each set of clues.

Clue Words			**Linking Words**
ware	quick	dollar	_____
bed	parent	file	_____
door	mouse	speed	_____
field	ship	plan	_____
age	testament	fashioned	_____

RAT Race

···

Your score for this round: _____

Directions: Find the best common linking word for each set of clues.

Clue Words			**Linking Words**
slot	vending	made	_____
television	primary	off	_____
hill	shoot	thumbs	_____
book	cuffs	back	_____
severance	roll	back	_____

RAT Race

···

Your score for this round: _____

Directions: Find the best common linking word for each set of clues.

Clue Words			**Linking Words**
bar	Caesar	bowl	_____
pipe	talks	corps	_____
flash	sore	breaking	_____
spring	music	ballot	_____
dragon	horse	swatter	_____

RAT Race

· ·

Your score for this round: _____

Directions: Find the best common linking word for each set of clues.

Clue Words			**Linking Words**
paper	letter	bad	_____
open	mat	bell	_____
safety	wheel	hat	_____
birth	first	fire	_____
mark	store	open	_____

RAT Race

· ·

Your score for this round: _____

Directions: Find the best common linking word for each set of clues.

Clue Words			**Linking Words**
alarm	side	drill	_____
grease	spray	job	_____
rocking	wheel	person	_____
motion	poke	down	_____
favor	birthday	pooper	_____

Regards

· ·

● PURPOSE

- To promote intra-group positive feedback and spontaneous acts of kindness.

- To demonstrate the self-fulfilling effect of positive comments on a working team.

● TIME

Ten minutes.

● PLAYERS

Any number.

● SUPPLIES

- An overhead transparency or newsprint flip-chart page of the Player Instructions for Regards, prepared in advance by the facilitator.

- An overhead projector (if using a transparency).

- Several sets of felt-tipped markers of various colors.

- Number 10 envelopes, one for each participant, and one for the facilitator.

- Paper and pencils for participants.

- Masking tape and thumb tacks or push pins.

- Large poster-sized sheet, such as the cardboard back from a newsprint pad, or a large bulletin board.

● STEPS

1. Distribute paper and pencils and give one envelope to each participant. Distribute one set of markers to each group of participants.

2. Define the task: "This is an affirmation exercise. First, fill out the back (the non-address side) of the envelope you received with your name and any design you wish. You may use various colored felt-tipped markers to decorate your envelope. Second, you will post your envelopes with the flap open [in the space designated]. Then, at any time during this session, you may place a note in another participant's envelope."

3. Have participants fill out their envelopes.

4. Post the Player Instructions, and discuss the recommended format of the note, given below.

   I [honor, thank you, appreciate, respect you for . . ., value, prize, am refreshed by . . .]

   because . . . [the reason].

   Signature (optional)

   Caution participants not to ask for anything in return from the person to whom they are giving affirmation. Asking for a favor turns praise into a commercial transaction.

5. Post the envelopes by tacking or taping them to the cardboard sheet or a large bulletin board with their flaps open and the decorated side with the name out.

● FACILITATOR NOTES

- Regards effectively demonstrates the value of thanking one another. A simple thank you helps to oil the gears of interpersonal relations. The better the interpersonal relations, the better the team.

- People may grumble about decorating their envelopes. Tell them that it is "refrigerator art" that they can take home at the end of the session and put on their refrigerators.

- After the participants have decorated and hung their envelopes, ask them to tear a sheet of paper into four pieces. Each piece can be used to write an affirmation. The smaller sheets of paper makes the task seem more doable for many participants.

- At first, participants may think that this is a worthless exercise, but if you try to stop the exercise at any point, most people will request that it continue. Everyone likes praise.

- You, as the facilitator, should also write affirmations for various members of the team. It is a good idea to write at least one for each person. Just make sure that the affirmation is real. If the person has not done anything worthy of praise, then do not write one.

● CUSTOMIZING REGARDS

Regarding Group Size

- Group size is not a factor. This can be played with any size group.

Regarding the Focus of the Task

- Encourage participation by giving the group time a few minutes before breaks and before lunch to fill out their notes.

- Encourage participation by giving the group time between lessons to fill out their notes.

- Have the participants practice this for a couple of days and then not do it for a couple of days. Compare the results.

Regards

- Decorate an envelope and place it on the wall.

- At any time, place an affirming note in any other partici-pant's envelope.

- Recommended structure of the note:

I

(honor, thank, appreciate, respect, value, prize, am refreshed by)

you

for . . .

because . . .

(describe the benefit to you or to the team).

Signature (optional)

Sentence Prompt

● ●

● **PURPOSE**

- To aid in planning and prioritizing activities.

- To promote group feedback.

- To receive instant group feedback on a problem statement or task.

- To create on-the-spot dialogue.

- To receive individual feedback on important issues or problems.

● **TIME**

Twenty minutes.

● **PLAYERS**

Ten or more.

● **SUPPLIES**

- An overhead transparency or newsprint flip-chart page of the Player Instructions for Sentence Prompt, prepared in advance by the facilitator.

- An overhead projector (if using a transparency).

- A newsprint flip chart and felt-tipped markers.

- A set of sentence prompts. (Sample Incomplete Statements for Sentence Prompt are provided at the end of this activity.)

- One set of 3″ x 5″ index cards or 3″ x 3″ Post-it® Notes and a pencil for each player.

- Masking tape.

- One set of self-sticking colored dots or symbols in at least four different colors.

● STEPS

1. Divide the group into teams of four to six players each.

2. Post an appropriate sentence prompt on the flip chart.

   Sample statement: "The most important task of this group is. . . ."

3. Distribute one set of Post-it® Notes or index cards and a pencil to each team member.

4. Define the task: "Each team has five minutes to come up with as many completions to this statement as it can. Each completion should be put on a separate Post-it® Note or index card. Your team will receive 1 point for each completion."

5. Post the Player Instructions, and begin the game.

6. After five minutes call time and award 1 point for each response.

7. Have each team post its notes on a different sheet of newsprint on a vertical surface.

8. Have teams review their notes and select the three or four most important themes.

9. Assign a different color dot to each of these themes.

10. With help from each team, place the appropriate color dot on its notes.

11. Award 3 points to each note that receives a colored dot.

12. Total each team's points. Declare the team with the most points the winner.

● FACILITATOR NOTES

- This is a productive exercise to help a team to sort out and publish issues that may be causing confusion. Sometimes it takes a lot of time for each member to state what he or she wants. Using this game the team can quickly see what is on everyone's mind and what the priority areas are.

- This activity can also allow team members to publish data anonymously. For example, it is a good way to address unspoken norms on the team.

- This exercise could also be played by a cyber team. Each member would send his or her completions to a trusted third party. That person would sort and categorize the sentence completions, then post a summary back to the whole group so that the group could prioritize the issues.

● CUSTOMIZING SENTENCE PROMPT

Regarding Group Size

- For smaller groups have individuals, rather than teams, post their completions to the sentence prompts. Then score one point for each response.

Regarding Time

- Shorten or lengthen time devoted to the exercise, as needed.

Regarding Scoring

- Establish a standard for a five-minute session, such as four responses per minute, for a "par" of twenty. Use the par to challenge smaller groups or as a guideline for teams with a new statement.

Regarding the Focus of the Task

- Break down a problem statement into sentence prompts. Divide the group into teams. Give each team a sentence prompt and have it complete the statement. Have each team present its responses to the rest of the group and then combine the answers, looking for feasible solutions.

- Present a proposed group decision in the form of a sentence prompt. Have individuals write down their responses and submit them. Collect the cards and present the collective individual input to the group. Sample statement: "The next major task this group should focus on is. . . ."

- Present a sentence prompt at any time, especially after a break, when feedback is desired on a specific process or topic. Sample statement: "The one topic I wish I could learn more about is. . . ." Ask for volunteers to share their responses. Record statements on a flip chart.

Sentence Prompt

....

- ## Divide into teams.

- ## Develop responses to incomplete sentences.

- ## Receive 1 point for each completion.

- ## Review and classify responses according to theme.

- ## Receive 3 point for each response that fits into one of the categories.

SAMPLE INCOMPLETE STATEMENTS FOR
Sentence Prompt

....

1. The most important task for this group is....

2. The best use of our time today would be....

3. The worst thing that could happen to this group is....

4. The best feature of our new product is....

5. The next step in solving our problem should be....

6. To solve this problem, we need to know more information about....

7. To make this solution work, we need the following resources....

8. This idea would succeed if we could only change....

9. The best thing that could happen to this group is....

10. The one thing that concerns me about this project is....

11. I would like to hear more input from....

12. I believe it will take our team about [hours, days, or weeks] to solve this problem.

Jossey-Bass/Pfeiffer

Snow Ball

. . . .

● PURPOSE

- To give immediate feedback on negative or unacceptable statements.

- To gauge the effect of immediate feedback on group behavior.

- To demonstrate the effectiveness and productivity of immediate feedback.

● TIME

Ten minutes.

● PLAYERS

Any number.

● SUPPLIES

- An overhead transparency or newsprint flip-chart page of the Player Instructions for Snow Ball, prepared in advance by the facilitator.

- An overhead projector (if using a transparency).

- List of Sample Killer Statements, provided at the end of this activity.

- Several pieces of scrap paper for each participant.

● STEPS

1. Introduce the list of sample "killer statements."

2. Ask participants whether they can add any killer statements to the list.

3. Ask each participant to wad a few pieces of scrap paper into "snow balls."

4. Ask for a volunteer. Tell the participants it will be painless.

5. Take the volunteer out of the room and explain that when you make a killer statement you would like him or her to toss a paper "snow ball" at you.

6. Return to the room without the volunteer and discuss with the group a suggestion or comment they could make to the volunteer.

7. Ask the volunteer to come back into the room.

8. Ask one of the participants to make a suggestion.

9. You then make a killer statement.

10. The volunteer should then throw the "snow ball" at you.

11. Post the Player Instructions for Snow Ball, and tell the group: "For the remainder of this session, when anyone, including me, makes a comment that you find offensive or disruptive, make a 'snow ball' and toss it at the offender immediately following the statement."

● FACILITATOR NOTES

- The purpose of this game is to show that feedback given right after something has been said or done is more effective than not giving the feedback or holding onto it for any length of time.

- If you do not want to let the participants toss paper at you, then do not even think of using this exercise. Everyone must be eligible for feedback.

- If you are having guest speakers, let them know what is happening.

- After a few hours or a day, here are some questions to ask to help the team focus on the topic of feedback:

  How do you feel when you throw a snow ball? What does it do for you?

  How do you feel about being hit by snow balls?

Has this experience fostered further discussion of what occurred?

Do you still feel any negative emotions about anything that was said or done? (In theory, if a discussion took place after the throwing, both thrower and receiver should feel that an understanding has been reached and not feel defensive or hostile.)

What does this exercise say about the importance of immediate feedback?

How could you implement this idea at work?

● CUSTOMIZING SNOWBALL

Regarding the Focus of the Task

- Have teams brainstorm how to solve a common problem and have people throw snow balls at killer statements.

- Every time a snow ball is tossed, collect it and place it in a special receptacle. At the end of the session, underscore the number of disruptive or unproductive statements by pointing to the receptacle.

- Assign a recorder to document each statement that earned a snow ball. Have the recorder present a list of these statements at the end of the program.

Regarding Scoring

- Have the player who is the target of the most snow balls collect and deposit all of them into a trash receptacle.

Snowball

- Toss wadded paper "snow balls" at anyone who makes a "killer" statement.

- The toss must immediately follow the statement.

- Discuss each occurrence, as needed.

Snow Ball

1. Yes, but. . . .

2. We don't have the people to do it!

3. It'll never fly!

4. It's not in the budget.

5. We tried that before and it didn't work.

6. I'm not the one who gets paid to think.

7. What will [name of person] think?

8. If it ain't broke, don't fix it!

9. Put it in writing.

10. It's all right in theory, but. . . .

11. It's not in my job description!

12. _____

13. _____

14. _____

15. _____

16. _____

17. _____

18. _____

Jossey-Bass/Pfeiffer

Super Model

. . . .

● PURPOSE

- To learn the planning and communication skills needed for a multi-team project.

- To explore the interaction and cooperation skills needed for a multi-team project.

- To practice problem solving in a multi-team environment.

● TIME

Forty minutes.

● PLAYERS

Twelve or more.

● SUPPLIES

- An overhead transparency or newsprint flip-chart page of the Player Instructions for Super Model, prepared in advance by the facilitator.

- An overhead transparency or newsprint flip-chart page of the Team Definitions for Super Model, prepared in advance by the facilitator.

- An overhead projector (if using transparencies).

- A copy of the Instructions for the Executive Council.

- A copy of the Instructions for the Sales Team.

- A copy of the Instructions for the Production Teams for each production team.

- A newsprint flip chart and at least one red and one blue felt-tipped marker for each team.

- One bag of miniature marshmallows for each team.

- One box of toothpicks for each team.

- A pair of scissors for each team.

- Masking tape for each team.

- Paper and pencils for each participant.

- A timer.

- An instant-process, digital, or video camera (optional).

- Play money, poker chips, or tokens (optional).

● STEPS

1. Divide the group into four or more teams of two to four players each.

2. Designate one team the Executive Council, one team the Sales Team, and the rest of the teams Production Teams.

3. Display or post the Team Definitions and define the task, "The Executive Council is to assist in the production and sales of an ornament for July 4th. The Executive Council will pick a company name and allocate all supplies. The Executive Council will also determine the bonus for the Production Team that produces the winning ornament.

   The Sales Team is to design a marketing plan for the July 4th ornament. The Sales Team will pick which product it will market, name the product, and serve as quality control during production.

   The Production Teams are to produce an ornament to be sold over the July 4th holiday. The Production Team that produces the product eventually selected will receive a bonus.

4. Give the following supplies to the Executive Council:

a. Miniature marshmallows

b. Toothpicks

c. Scissors

d. Felt-tipped markers

e. Masking tape

f. Paper and pencils

g. Play money, poker chips, or tokens (optional)

5. Post the Player Instructions, distribute the appropriate Instruction Sheets to each team, answer any questions, and begin the game.

6. Ask the Executive Council to name the company by the end of the first round.

7. *Round 1.* Have the Production Teams design their ornaments. Call time when all production teams have completed their designs. (You may also call time if one or two production teams are very slow and far behind the other teams.) If teams are close to completion, then allow them to finish.

(Another point at which to call time is if the Executive Council has not distributed the supplies to all Production Teams after about thirty minutes. If this is the situation, then there is a problem in organizational communication that needs to be addressed before the game can continue.)

8. Ask the Executive Council to present the company name.

9. *Round 2.* Ask each team to present its ornament and to describe its features and benefits. (Take a picture of each ornament and the presentation if using an instant or digital camera or a video recorder.)

10. Ask the Sales Team to select the model of the ornament that they would like to sell. Have the Sales Team pick a name for the product.

11. Ask the Executive Council to award a bonus to the Production Team that produced the winning ornament.

12. *Round 3.* Ask the Sales Team to present its marketing plan for the ornament.

13. *Round 4.* Ask each Production Team to produce as many of the ornament that was selected as they can in ten or fifteen minutes. The Sales Team will serve as the quality control function and accept or reject each ornament. Only ornaments that match the winning model exactly should be accepted.

14. Call time after ten or fifteen minutes. Ask the Sales Team to determine which Production Team has produced the most acceptable ornaments.

15. Ask the Executive Council to present a bonus to that Production Team.

● FACILITATOR NOTES

- You may use any holiday for this activity.

- This game is useful when teams rely on one another to produce a product or service on the job. It provides an excellent opportunity to study the interaction between teams and among team members.

- It is very important that time be spent reaching agreement on what happened during the first step in the debriefing process. Not every person will have seen or heard what happened on the other teams. Therefore, before the participants can start drawing lessons from their play, they have to know everything that happened. During this stage do not allow the members to talk about the meaning of what happened, their intentions, and so forth. Make sure the participants stick to what was done and what was said only.

- Super Model calls for close cooperation among teams. Each team must interact well with the other teams if the task is to be accomplished. When debriefing this game it is suggested that you use the following sequence:

  Have each team rate its own efficiency and effectiveness and write their rating on a flip chart.

  Have each team rate the efficiency and effectiveness of the other teams.

  Select one team to go first and have that team present its own rating of itself and its rationale to the entire group.

  Have the other teams reveal their evaluations of that team. Facilitate the discussion so that positive outcomes are achieved. Continue this process for the other teams.

  Once all teams have presented their ratings, received feedback, and discussed their performance, have each team answer the following question: "What can we do back on the job to capture some of the lessons we have learned?" After all teams have answered this question, ask them to share their answers with the whole group. Prioritize the lessons learned and make implementation plans.

- Use the following questions to address the question of rewards:

  What was the effect on your performance of working for a bonus? (This question will provide the teams with an opportunity to discuss effective rewards for performance.)

  Did those choosing the reward consider asking those receiving the reward whether it would be considered a reward or not?

  How should rewards for team production be determined?

- If you use an intact team for this game, pose the following questions:

  How did your behavior in this game mirror your behavior back on the job?

  Were the results you achieved here any different from the results you achieve back at work? In what way?

  Does the way you communicated during this game hold any lessons for you on the job?

  What are some effective ways for team members to let each other know what they need from one another to be effective in their jobs?

  What could you do differently back at work to improve your interactions with one another?

- To debrief this game, start with the teams themselves first, the interaction between the teams second, and then the behavior of the whole organization. There are different lessons to be learned for each level of the organization.

- When you are debriefing the behavior of the whole organization some useful questions to ask are:

  What was the effect of competition on the productivity of the organization as a whole?

  What was the effect of cooperation on the productivity of the organization as a whole?

  How can we manage competition so as not to hinder the mission of the organization?

● CUSTOMIZING SUPER MODEL

Regarding Group Size

- No team should have fewer than two members or more than six members.

Regarding Time

- Given the complexities of this game, imposing time limits could result in complaints from the players that the reason they could not perform better was because of the imposed time limits. This could cause major problems during the debriefing.

Regarding the Focus of the Task

- Vary the materials by adding colored paper, paper clips, buttons, and empty egg cartons to the supplies given to the Executive Council.

- Add more complexity to the task by introducing additional teams, for instance:

  A Budget Team to approve a materials budget for the Production Teams.

  A Supply Team to pass out materials and set limits for the supplies available during each round of play.

  A Customer Team to decide whether or not to buy the product.

- Place each team in a separate room to determine how distance affects inter-team communication, cooperation, and decision making.

- Use any holiday for the ornament.

Super Model

- **Divide into appropriate teams.**

- **Round 1:**

  Design ornament

  Create a company name

- **Round 2:**

  Present model ornaments

  Select best ornament model

  Create a product name

  Award bonus to winning team

- **Round 3:**

  Present the marketing plan

- **Round 4:**

  Produce the selected ornament

  Select team with most products

  Award bonus to winning team

INSTRUCTIONS FOR THE EXECUTIVE COUNCIL FOR
Super Model

Executives have many and varied tasks in an organization. The main task of the Executive Council is to make sure that the company is moving in a predetermined direction. It is the mission of the Executive Council for Super Model to guide the sales and production of a new ornament for the 4th of July.

Some of the problems facing the Executive Council are:

- The company has no name.

- A bonus plan must be determined.

- The supply distribution system has broken down.

- There is no marketing plan for the 4th of July ornament.

- There is no model of the 4th of July ornament.

- Competition for supplies is reported to be fiercely competitive among the production teams.

- There appears to be some hostility between Sales and Production.

You may also have to perform tasks that are not listed in these instructions. The proper performance of your tasks is your decision. If you think something needs to be done, proceed with it in an effective and efficient manner.

Jossey-Bass/Pfeiffer

Super Model

Currently the organization is trying to design and produce an ornament for the 4th of July. It is the mission of the Sales Team to market, sell, and provide quality control on the production of ornaments produced by the Production Teams.

Some of the problems facing the Sales Team are:

- Finding a suitable model for a 4th of July ornament.

- Selecting a name for the ornament.

- Devising a marketing/sales plan and obtaining Executive Council approval for it.

- Pricing the 4th of July ornament.

- Solving quality problems on the Production Teams.

You may also have to perform tasks that are not listed in these instructions. The proper performance of your tasks is your decision. If you think something needs to be done, proceed with it in an effective and efficient manner.

INSTRUCTIONS FOR THE PRODUCTION TEAMS FOR
Super Model

It is the mission of the Production Teams to design and produce a model for a 4th of July ornament. Once one of the designs is selected for rollout, the Production Teams must produce sufficient quantity of the ornament to meet demand.

Some of the problems facing the Production Teams are:

- A 4th of July ornament must be designed.

- There are rumors of a scarcity of supplies.

- The models must be presented to the Executive Council and Sales Team for approval.

- Once approval is given, as many ornaments as possible must be produced that match the model exactly.

- Teams are in competition for the bonuses for producing the winning model and for exceeding production quotas.

- The Sales Team seems to be very strict when determining quality.

You may also have to perform tasks that are not listed in these instructions. The proper performance of your tasks is your decision. If you think something needs to be done, proceed with it in an effective and efficient manner.

TEAM DEFINITIONS FOR
Super Model

- The Executive Council is to assist in the production and sales of a July 4th ornament. The Executive Council will pick the name of the company and allocate all supplies. It will also determine the bonus for the Production Team that produces the winning ornament and the bonus for producing the most product.

- The Sales Team is to design a marketing plan for a July 4th ornament. It will pick the product that will be marketed, name the product, and also serve in a quality control function while overseeing production of the product.

- The Production Teams are to design prototypes of a product that will be sold over the July 4th holiday. The Production Team that produces the most of the product selected by the Sales Team will receive a bonus, and the team whose design is selected will receive a bonus.

Team Roast

● PURPOSE

- To identify characteristics of effective and ineffective teams.

- To help participants transition to the topic under discussion.

● TIME

Twenty-five minutes.

● PLAYERS

Twelve or more.

● SUPPLIES

- An overhead transparency or newsprint flip-chart page of the Player Instructions for Team Roast, prepared in advance by the facilitator.

- An overhead projector (if using a transparency).

- A newsprint flip chart and felt-tipped markers.

- One sheet of newsprint and markers for each team.

- Masking tape.

- Paper and pencils for each participant.

- One ballot for each player. (A Player's Ballot for Team Roast is provided at the end of this game.)

● STEPS

1. Divide the group into three or more teams of four to six players each. Have each team sit at a table.

2. Distribute one sheet of newsprint, strips of masking tape, felt-tipped markers, paper, and pencils to each team.

3. Illustrate the concept of dramatizing statements made about teams in the form of song titles, movie titles, book titles, bumper stickers, slogans, names of television shows, headlines, or epitaphs, as in the following examples:

   a. Epitaph for an ineffective team: "Here Lies Our Team Titanic; First They Bungled, Then They Panicked."

   b. Television game show title for an ineffective team: "Family Feud."

   c. Movie title for an effective team: "A Team for All Seasons."

4. Define the task for Round 1: "You will have ten minutes to develop ten dramatic statements about teams—five statements about an effective team and five statements about an ineffective team. Write your ten statements on the sheet of newsprint provided."

5. Display the Player Instructions, and start the game.

6. After ten minutes, call time. Have each team post its newsprint list on the wall.

7. Distribute one ballot to each player.

8. Define the task for Round 2: "Each player has five minutes to review other teams' lists and vote for the three best individual items from any team's list. Cast one vote each for (1) the most profound, (2) the most unique, and (3) the most humorous."

9. After five minutes, call time and collect the ballots.

10. Sort the votes by category; then award 1 point to the team that created each statement selected.

11. Tally the final score. The team with the most points wins.

● FACILITATOR NOTES

- The lists produced during this activity can be used later to process other activities. For example, after an activity ask the participants to list what occurred and then see whether they fall under the definition of an effective or an ineffective team.

- This activity can also be used to give you an idea of what the participants' thinking is regarding teams. Using this information you can talk about:

  The power of expectations. If you think something they do will lead to poor teamwork, you may decide to allow that bad situation by not challenging the team to look for an alternative and then using the situation as an example.

  The definition of teams. It is important to be clear right at the beginning about the types of teams you are going to be talking about and the types of teams you will not cover.

- You can also use this activity to refer back to when talking about the various traits of teams. When talking about team activities that produce good results, refer back to the list of good traits. When talking about activities that produce bad results, go back to the list of poor traits. You can also point out techniques that are good alternatives and discuss how to achieve them.

- The following are suggested questions to process the activity. Substitute other questions to focus on a specific topic you want to discuss.

  What similarities do you see in the teams' lists?

  What differences do you see in the teams' lists?

  What do those similarities and differences mean?

  Can we draw any conclusions about teams from these lists?

  How could we use this information with our teams back at work?

● CUSTOMIZING TEAM ROAST

Regarding Group Size

- For groups smaller than twelve, divide into three teams of two or more per team.

Regarding Time

- Shorten or lengthen rounds of play, as needed.

Regarding the Focus of the Task

- Have teams prepare a skit portraying one or more team characteristic. Have other teams vote on "best presentation."

Team Roast

- Write five statements about effective teams and five statements about ineffective teams.

- Post your team's statements on the wall.

- Vote for your three favorite statements.

- Win points for statements selected.

Team Roast

. . . .

1. Most Profound: _____

2. Most Unique: _____

3. Most Humorous: _____

Jossey-Bass/Pfeiffer

Tooth and Nail

•••

● PURPOSE

- To demonstrate differences between cooperation and competition.

- To explore the effect of a competitive environment on intra-team cooperation.

- To demonstrate the principles of negotiating.

● TIME

Twenty minutes.

● PLAYERS

Eight or more.

● SUPPLIES

- An overhead transparency or newsprint flip-chart page of the Player Instructions for Tooth and Nail, prepared in advance by the facilitator.

- An overhead transparency or newsprint flip-chart page of the Payoff Matrix for Tooth and Nail, prepared in advance by the facilitator.

- An overhead transparency or newsprint flip-chart page of the Score Sheet for Tooth and Nail, prepared in advance by the facilitator.

- An overhead projector (if using transparencies).

- A newsprint flip chart and felt-tipped markers.

- One tooth picture card and one nail picture card per team, prepared in advance by the facilitator. (Cards that can be copied and cut apart are provided at the end of this game.)

- One copy of the Score Sheet and a pencil per team.

● STEPS

1. Divide the group into sets of two teams of three or more players each. Have each set of teams face each other at a table.

2. Distribute two different picture cards, a pencil, and one Score Sheet to each team.

3. Define the task: "The object of this game is to collect as many points as you can over five rounds of play. Each round consists of a 'showdown' during which each team shows one of its cards to achieve a score determined by the Payoff Matrix. Each round is played in the same fashion."

4. Post the Player Instructions and the Payoff Matrix and begin the game. The Payoff Matrix should remain visible at all times.

5. Announce: "Teams ready? One, two, three . . . show your cards."

6. Have teams record their scores for both cards shown on the Payoff Matrix on the line for Round 1.

7. Continue play in this fashion for five rounds.

8. Stop play at the end of the fifth round. Have each set of teams tally scores and determine which team scored the most points.

● SCORING EXAMPLE

1. Team A versus Team B.

2. Facilitator announces: "Teams ready? One, two, three . . . show your cards." Team A shows the nail card; Team B shows the tooth card.

3. According to the Payoff Matrix, Team A receives 0 points and Team B receives 5 points. Both teams record their scores for Round 1 on the Score Sheet.

Round	Team A	Team B
1	0	5

This completes play for Round 1.

4. Facilitator announces: "Teams ready for Round 2? One, two, three . . . show your cards." Team A shows tooth; Team B shows tooth.

5. According to the Payoff Matrix, Team A receives 0 points and Team B receives 0 points. Both teams record their scores as follows:

Round	Team A	Team B
1	0	5
2	0	0

This completes play for Round 2.

6. Facilitator announces: "Teams ready for Round 3? One, two, three . . . show your cards." Team A shows nail and Team B shows nail.

7. According to the Payoff Matrix, Team A receives 3 points and Team B receives 3 points. Both teams record their scores for Round 3 as follows:

Round	Team A	Team B
1	0	5
2	0	0
3	3	3

This completes play for Round 3.

8. Play continues in this fashion through Round 5.

- Notice that the participants will undoubtedly substitute the words "more points than the other team" in place of the words that appear in the instructions, which are "as many points as possible." This game helps show how easily participants slip into competitive behavior. The game should help illustrate how participants have to work at being cooperative.

  Further explore this issue by asking the participants how they react to working with another team, especially on a project that could have positive or negative consequences.

- Teams will also think in terms of win-lose, rather than win-win.

- Negotiation sessions can be offered. You may find that teams that have scored more points than others will tend to choose *not* to negotiate during the rounds when negotiation is called for.

Some questions you can ask to help draw out the participants:

Why made you choose cooperation/competition?

What negotiation scenarios worked and which ones did not? Why was that?

If someone lied to you during negotiation, how did you react to that person?

How do you prepare to enter a negotiation session? Is the preparation the same or different depending on whether you are going to be negotiating with a friendly, unknown, or slightly hostile team?

What makes people on a team want to cooperate with one another or with another team?

- During the debriefing, ask each team to figure out the most points they could have earned if they had cooperated. How does that compare to what they have earned? Is cooperation the optimum solution for this activity?

- Explore how the teams could have encouraged the opposing team to cooperate.

- This game of choices and consequences reflects the well-known scenario portrayed in the classic game, "Prisoner's Dilemma," where two prisoners are jointly accused of a crime and must plead either "guilty" or "not guilty." If both prisoners plead guilty, they receive a heavy sentence. If both prisoners plead not guilty, they receive a lighter sentence. However, the prisoner who informs on his or her adversary receives a lighter sentence for pleading guilty than that person does for pleading not guilty.

● CUSTOMIZING TOOTH AND NAIL

Regarding Group Size

- Divide smaller groups into two teams.

Regarding Time

- Expand the rounds to seven or more, as needed.

Regarding Focus of the Task

- Increase the team size to five to seven players each. Have each team select a representative. For each round of play each representative meets first with his or her respective team, then the two representatives have a "showdown."

Regarding Scoring

- Announce that the scores will be doubled for the last round. See whether a change in scoring produces any different game strategies.

- After Rounds 2 and 4 allow the teams to negotiate with each other. Double the points for each round following inter-team negotiations.

- Increase or decrease the points in the Payoff Matrix.

- Introduce a third scoring option: a "no show," which costs the playing team 1 point, but allows no gain in points by its opponent. For example, Team A has 10 points, Team B has 7 points. Team A chooses to play "no show." No matter what Team B shows, the score following the round would be:

    Team B stays the same at 7 points

    Team A subtracts 1 point, for a total of $10 - 1 = 9$ points.

Tooth and Nail

Divide into sets of two teams.

Your team will try to collect as many points as possible.

• Each team receives one tooth and one nail card.

Round 1: Show one card.

Compute team scores according to the Payoff Matrix.

• Play is same for all rounds.

Tooth and Nail

Round	Team A	Team B
1		
2		
3		
4		
5		

Total Points

PAYOFF MATRIX FOR
Tooth and Nail

....

Points	Team A Shows	Team B Shows	Points
5	tooth	nail	0
0	nail	tooth	5
3	nail	nail	3
0	tooth	tooth	0

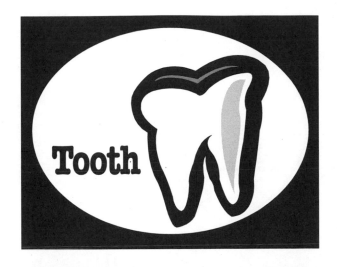

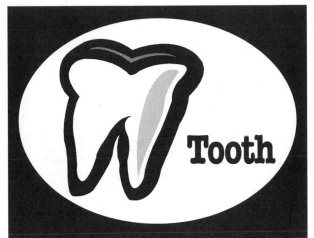

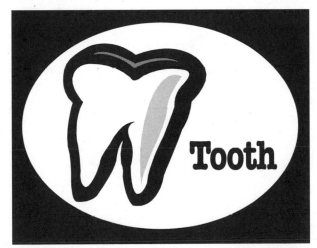

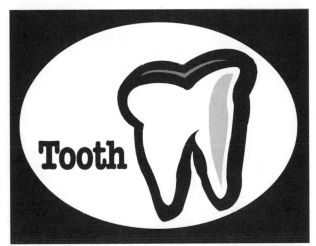

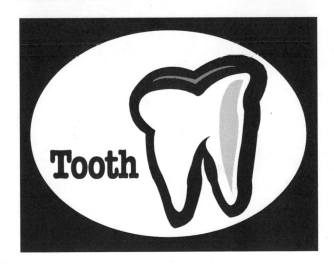

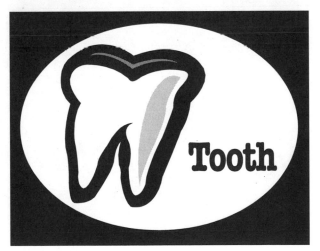

ww.where and ww.when

. . . .

● **PURPOSE**

- To provide an opportunity for people who work at a distance from one another to explore issues that impact on the productivity of a cyber team, such as conflict management, communication, decision making, information sharing, goal setting, prioritization of work, and trust.

● **TARGET AUDIENCE**

Members of a team who do not work in the same location.

● **PLAYERS**

Six to eight.

● **TIME**

Six days.

● **SUPPLIES/CAPABILITIES**

- Each player should be able to send to and receive e-mail from all the other members of the team and the facilitator.

- Each player and the facilitator should have access to an Internet browser such as Netscape Navigator® or Microsoft Explorer®. Having a browser will also enable the participants to search for information about conference facilities, airlines, car rentals, and so on on-line.

- (Optional) On-line conferencing capability.

● STEPS

- Send a message to the players informing them about any chat and conferencing functions they will be expected to use. Ask the players to respond by providing you with their e-mail addresses.

Task One: Pick a Team Leader

- E-mail the players and ask them to select a team leader. Give them a deadline by which to make their selection and notify you.

Task Two: Send Memo to Team Leader

- Send the following memo to the team leader via e-mail. Feel free to modify the memo in any way that will make this task more real for the participants. The point is to research and agree on arrangements for an imaginary conference as a team.

To: [Team Leader's Name]

From: [Facilitator's Name]

Subject: Planning for Conference on [Topic]

Date: [Date Memo Sent]

Congratulations! You and your team have been chosen to coordinate the upcoming conference on [topic] that will take place in [city] and run from [date] to [date].

You have five months to plan this conference. For the purposes of this activity, every day will be considered one month. The clock will start tonight at midnight [your time zone]. By [date that is five days from when you send the memo] you should have the conference fully planned. You are expected to present this plan to me on [day after the deadline].

Here is some information that will help you accomplish your planning task. The list is not intended to be exhaustive, but simply to spark your thinking.

1. Expected attendance is 2,000 people.
2. Most of the meals will be supplied on site, with some mealtimes left open for participants to explore eateries in the host city.
3. Accommodations must be user friendly for disabled people.
4. Accommodations must be made for those who have special dietary needs.
5. Most people will fly into the city and may or may not need rental cars.
6. The host hotels should be close to the conference center.
7. Fee structure should allow for both full and partial attendance. Consider offering a discount registration fee package and determine whether there will be various deadlines for registering.
8. Determine how you will select speakers, whether they will be paid and how much, and whether their hotel stays, meals, and air fare will be gratis.
9. Address how you will select vendors who display their products and services at the conference. What will you charge them? Will that charge include hotel, air travel, meals, and conference registration?
10. Will you have committees and, if so, what are they and how will they be selected?
11. Will there be an option for the conference to be on-line for those who cannot attend in person?

Any clarifications should be addressed to me. Letters you send to hypothetical vendors, speakers, or suppliers should also be sent to me for a response.

Thank you and remember that I am here to help you through the process. My e-mail address is [supply address].

Task Three: Respond to Questions

- If the team invites you to participate in an on-line conference, feel free to do so. What information you give them is up to you.

- If the team is moving along at a good pace and seems to be accomplishing its tasks, you might want to answer the questions sent to you with information that would present a roadblock to the team, which could help the team learn how to work under adverse conditions.

- If the team is fumbling with the task, then you might want to answer questions in such a way as to help the team with its process.

- In either case, do not do the team's work or tell the team how to proceed.

Task Four: Send Vendor E-Mail

- Send the following e-mail message to the team leader on the afternoon of the second day.

To: [Team Leader]

From: [Your Name]

Subject: Selection of Vendors

Date:

I received a call this afternoon from Vendor X, who was very concerned that his company would not have an opportunity to participate in the conference you are planning. I told him that I was unaware that any vendors were being excluded. Am I correct in that assumption?

Please e-mail me your suggested response to Vendor X no later than tonight.

Thank you.

Task Five: Hotel Query

- By the afternoon of the third day, if you have not received an e-mail from the team concerning hotel reservations, send the team leader the following memo:

> **To:** [Team Leader]
>
> **From:** [Your Name]
>
> **Subject:** Hotel Reservations
>
> **Date:**
>
> I have been informed by the Hotel Association of [city] that discount rooms are no longer available for our conference. It seems that you waited too long to make final arrangements with any of the hotels in [city].
>
> Please confirm by e-mail if this is correct and what you have accomplished so far.

Task Six: Airline Arrangements

- By the afternoon of the fourth day, if you have not heard from the team about airline arrangements, send the following memo:

> **To:** [Team Leader]
>
> **From:** [Your Name]
>
> **Subject:** Airline Reservations
>
> **Date:**
>
> I have been informed by the Airline Association that discount fares are no longer available for the time of our conference. You waited too long to make final arrangements with the airlines.
>
> Please confirm by return e-mail if this is a correct reflection of what you have accomplished so far.

Task Seven: Debriefing

- On the morning of the sixth day, the day after the session is over, send an e-mail to the team informing them of the time and date for a debriefing of the activity. Share with the team some of the questions you plan to ask. Also, solicit any questions that they would like to ask.

● FACILITATOR NOTES

- Debriefing of this game works best if done in person; next best if done in an on-line conferencing setting; third best by e-mail.

- If you receive an e-mail from anyone on the team, whether the team leader or a team member, always ask if you should "cc:" the rest of the team with your answer. One of the problems that cyber teams experience is a shortage of shared information. When a team is working together in an office setting, members pick up information through interaction with one another. A cyber team has to work harder at sharing information. By asking them if they want you to "cc:" the rest of the team members, you can encourage them to think about how they share information.

- You may hear complaints from the participants if there are problems with the computer software, hardware, or telecommunications media. Ask the team members to focus on what *is* working, rather than what is not, and on how to achieve their goal with what is available. Remind them that a computer system/network always seems to have something wrong with it and waiting until everything is working perfectly may be a very long wait.

  If the team reports computer problems, remind them that they are not the first people to have such problems. Ask them to research how others have solved the problem. Resist the temptation to become the technical expert for the team.

- Ask the following question of the team: "What critical factors impact the effectiveness of cyber teams?" As they answer, summarize the various issues and topics and provide feedback, discussing ways to handle these problems in the future. Ask how the issues affected their teamwork and what they will do in the future to prevent the problem from recurring.

- Some other questions that will help the team focus on its specific behavior during the activity follow:

  How did you pick a team leader?

  How did you divide up the tasks?

  What process did you use to prioritize tasks?

  Did everyone participate?

  What goals did you set for the team?

  What process did you use to make decisions?

Jossey-Bass/Pfeiffer

How did you share information with one another? Did you set up mailing lists? Did you cc: one another?

How did you handle disagreements on your team?

What issues do you need to pay attention to so that your cyber team works.

What team practices do you plan to establish as a result of playing this game?

● CUSTOMIZING WW.WHERE AND WW.WHEN

Regarding Group Size

- If you are working with an actual team, then the size of the team will be pre-determined.

- If you are conducting a training session and have to form the teams, keep team size to no more than eight participants each.

Regarding Time

- Shorten or lengthen time of play by deleting or adding compressed days to the schedule.

- Run the game over a longer time period to allow participants to complete the game along with their regular work activities.

Regarding the Focus of the Task

- Add additional tasks or provide guidance, as necessary.

- Vary the assignment by adding special tasks, such as tours of the host city or special security for a selected speaker.

- Vary the audience requirements by having the group provide accommodations for the sight, sound, and physically challenged.

- Have the team send you a short e-mail at the end of each day that summarizes what was accomplished that day.

- Have the team report on the technical requirements of the speakers, such as overhead transparencies, flip charts, white boards, laptop computers, Internet connections, e-mail capability, pull-down screens, or conference calling capability.

About the Authors

∙∙∙

Steve Sugar, M.B.A., is the president of The Game Group and a writer and teacher in the use of learning games. He is the author of *Games That Teach* (Jossey-Bass/Pfeiffer) and the developer of three game systems used across the world (HRD Press). Sugar has been interviewed by *Personnel Journal, Training & Development* and *TRAINING* magazines. He is a speaker at all of the major training conferences and an editor-contributor on several (ASTD) *INFO-LINE* publications; contributor of chapters on game design for *The ASTD Handbook of Instructional Technology* and *The ASTD Handbook of Training Design*; and contributor to the *Team and Organization Development Sourcebook* (McGraw-Hill) and *The 2000 Annual, Volume 2 Consulting* (Jossey-Bass/Pfeiffer).

George J. Takacs, who earned his master's degree from the University of Notre Dame, has more than 30 years of management, training, and consulting experience in the private, not-for-profit, and public sectors. Takacs first started building teams in 1979 while he working at the Bureau of the Mint. He has been building self-directed work teams since 1990. Over the past three years he has been working with cyber teams. Takacs teaches courses in organization development and problem solving over the Internet for the University of Maryland, University College. He also presents courses over the Internet for university faculty on how to teach on the Internet. His firm, Takacs Techniques, has its own Web-based classroom used to present classes, conferences, and coaching to managers and executives. Takacs has presented at many national and regional conferences on such topics as organizational change, customer service, and slaying your dragons. He has also published articles in the areas of organizational change and customer service.

Two training legends offer you a definitive team sourcebook!

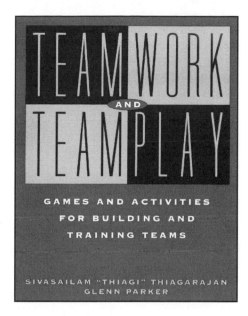

Sivasailam "Thiagi" Thiagarajan
& Glenn M. Parker

Teamwork and Teamplay

Games and Activities for Building and Developing Teams

The world's two best-known team-building facilitators bring you over thirty-five cutting-edge activities. Are you starting a new team? Are you working to improve the performance of a longstanding team? You'll turn to this treasury of hassle-free, sure-fire games, exercises, and simulations time and time again.

"In keeping with the tradition of continuous learning about teamwork, Thiagi and Parker have hit a home run. *Teamwork and Teamplay* is a must-have for every training bookshelf."
—Harvey A. Robbins, co-author, Why Teams Don't Work

"I can think of forty reasons to buy this book: thirty-eight games and activities, each a gem plus two of the best writers in the training business. I am truly impressed at how well each activity is designed and how easy the rules are to understand."
—Steve Sugar, author, Games That Teach; president, The Game Group

"This book performs the real service of helping neophytes and experts alike to explore the factors that influence team effectiveness. Practitioners will use these games and activities to propel teams to peak performance."
—Danny Langdon, president, Performance International; co-editor, Intervention Resource Guide

"Anyone who is leading, facilitating, or working in teams—and these days, who isn't?—will find clear instructions and powerful activities from two internationally recognized experts in the field."
—Diane Dormant, president, Dormant & Associates; past president, The International Society for Performance Improvement (ISPI)

"This is the book we've been waiting for! It deals with current topics, such as virtual teams, and with classic concepts, such as cultural transformation. There's an effective activity for every aspect of teamwork."
—Kathleen Whiteside, president, K.S. Whiteside and Associates; past president, ISPI; co-editor, Intervention Resource Guide

"Absolutely the best toolbox for teamwork I've seen. Anyone involved in training and facilitation should have this resource close at hand!"
—Gregory J. Kelble, BOC Process Systems

You'll use these games to develop skills in:

- Idea generation
- Self-directed teaming
- Consensus building
- Problem solving
- Conflict resolution . . . and much more!

The game formats are varied: some short, some long; some icebreakers, some closers; and much more. A game selection matrix enables you to find a game that suits your situation. Plus, training legends Thiagi and Parker share with you their proven insights on effective teamwork and facilitation.

About the Authors

Sivasailam "Thiagi" Thiagarajan is president of Workshops by Thiagi, a consulting and training company. He is also the editor of the *Thiagi GameLetter*, a newsletter that deals with training games and activities.

Glenn M. Parker author of *Team Players and Teamwork*, among other best-selling books is president of Glenn M. Parker & Associates, a training and consulting firm that works with organizations to create and sustain high-performing team-based systems.

paperback / 192 pages
• • • • • • • • • • • • • • • •
Teamwork and Teamplay
Item #G457

There are "teams" ... and then there are high-performing teams!

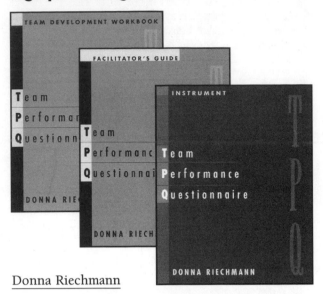

Donna Riechmann

Team Performance Questionnaire

You expect results from your work groups. You want high-performing teams, work groups that demonstrate superior, sustained performance. You want an assessment that shows work groups what they're doing right—and what they could do better. You want a quick but comprehensive program that shows groups how to use these assessments to develop their team skills.

It's all here! The *Facilitator's Guide* gives you all the information you need to run a team development program based on Donna Riechmann's *Team Performance Questionnaire (TPQ)*.

The *Facilitator's Guide* shows you how to:

- *Administer* the *TPQ*
- *Prepare* for and conduct a *TPQ* workshop
- *Develop* teams using results from the *TPQ* ... and more!

The field-tested, proven-effective *Team Performance Questionnaire (TPQ)* will boost your team's performance by offering you a clear path for growth. Participants will use the action-focused *Team Development Workbook* (included free with the *TPQ*) to score, analyze, and interpret the *TPQ* results. And filling out the *TPQ* is quick and easy!

The *TPQ* will:

- *Improve* team productivity
- *Enhance* team communication
- *Boost* team satisfaction ... and much more!

Give your teams the key to enhanced performance. Conduct a *TPQ* workshop at your organization!

Facilitator's Guide / paperback / 48 pages / includes one sample copy of Instrument • Instrument / 4 pages / includes one copy of Team Development Workbook (24 pages)

· · · · · · · · · · · ·

Facilitator's Guide
Item #F702

Instrument
Item #F701

Games are your answer!

Steve Sugar

Games That Teach

Experiential Activities for Reinforcing Training

Foreword by Sivasailam "Thiagi" Thiagarajan

They don't want to hear you lecture. They don't want to read an instruction guide. So how can you tell them what they need to know? You want bright smiles, not bored sighs. You want them to have fun, but you want them to learn as well. GAMES are your answer!

Games aren't just for kids. Games can help people learn business ideas: games can teach. Steve Sugar's adaptable designs put an end to tired, scripted business games. Sometimes you have a lot of games, but none of them ever seem to suit the occasion. Sometimes games suit the occasion, but are so rigid that the participants are bored before they've scarcely even begun. With Sugar's help, your games will always be both fitting and new. These designs are enjoyable, but they are also "games that teach"—every game has a practical, instructional purpose.

In this book you'll get:

- *An abundance of unique and playful games.* These content-reinforcing designs will increase the "smile quotient" of even the most hard-to-please audience.
- *A handy selection matrix.* This tool helps you choose the games that suit your specific training needs.
- *A simple seven-step game implementation model.* This plan shows you how to customize these designs for your own use.

As a student, Sugar used games to remember his schoolwork; as a teacher, he used games to energize dull lessons; as a trainer, he uses games to excite learners and accelerate learning. And now he offers you this invaluable treasury of his fluid game designs. Bring a bounty of frame game fun to your next training session or presentation!

paperback / 208 pages

· · · · · · · · · · · ·

Games That Teach
Item #F507
